MORE THAN JUST SEX

A Committed Couples Guide to Keeping Relationships Lively, Intimate & Gratifying

by Daniel Beaver, M.S., MFCC

Aslan Publishing
PO Box 108
Lower Lake, CA 95457

Published by

Aslan Publishing
P.O. Box 108
Lower Lake, CA 95457
(707) 995-1861

For a free catalog of all our titles,
or to order more copies of this book
please call (800) 275-2606

Library of Congress Cataloging-in-Publication Data:

Beaver, Daniel.
    More than just sex : a committed couples guide to keeping
relationships lively, intimate & gratifying / by Daniel Beaver.--
1st ed.
            p. cm.
    Includes bibliographical references.
    ISBN 0-944031-35-8 : $12.95
    1. Sex in marriage--United States. 2. Sex. 3. Intimacy
(Psychology) I. Title.
HQ18.U5B35 1992
306.7--dc20

Cover design by Laura Jump, Scott Lamorte and Brenda Plowman
Cover artwork produced by Scott Lamorte

Printed in USA
First Edition

10 9 8 7 6 5 4 3 2

Table of Contents

For my wife, Debra
and my two daughters, Danielle & Michelle

In memory of my mother,
Edith Ruth Beaver-Quinn
&
Michael Tobin, Ph.D.
John Wesley Laccoarce, M.S.
two of my best friends and colleagues

Acknowledgments

Many people have contributed to the eight-year evolution of this book. I would like to thank Thèa Lowry, M.A., and Tom Lowry, M.D., for all their help and training, and acknowledge my early co-therapists, Bonnie Darwin, B.A., Mary Mullen, M.S., and Sheilah Fish, M.A., for their insights. Allure Jeffcoat, M.S., a pioneer human sexuality teacher, gave me the opportunity to teach at the college level; Diane Beeson, Ph.D., Juan Gonzales, Ph.D., and Kris Hammer, M.A., allowed me the pleasure of lecturing in their classes.

Many people at the Relationship Counseling Center of Walnut Creek have given me guidance and support, including Janet Forman, M.A., Sheilah Fish, M.A., Michael Tobin, Ph.D., Wes Laccoarce, M.S., Bonnie Cameron, M.A., Teresa Welborn, D.A., Renee Baron, M.A., Dennis Lees, M.S.W., Philip Manfield, Ph.D., Hank Visscher, M.A., Anthony Newey, Ph.D., Stephen Polsky, Ph.D., Michael Levin, M.D., Ken Jones, M.S., Carol Scarborough, M.A., Julie Blunden-Schadlich, M.S., Sara Somers, M.S., Peter Oppermann, Ph.D., Gail Kinsley-Dame, M.A., Elaine Groen, R.D., and Sue Coffee. Special thanks to Hal Zina Bennett and Richard Heinberg for their work on this book.

I appreciate my family's encouragement and support of my goal of getting published again, especially my brother, Robert Elliot, whose feedback was always there. I am most grateful for the love and continued support of Drs. George and Mae McAuley, and Glenn Quinn. Thanks to the staff of Aslan Publishing: Dawson Church, Brenda Plowman, Jenny D'Angelo, for seeing the potential of my manuscript and giving it your creative support.

Lastly, I want to thank Debra Ellen Keyson, the best lover, friend, and wife a man could ever desire. Your love and support have given me the strength and conviction to write this book. You made it possible for me to take all my intellectual concepts and truly experience what it means to be intimate. I'm grateful for the love and inspiration provided by my daughters, Danielle and Michelle. My hope is that this book will help you, as adults, to experience intimate, healthy relationships.

—Daniel Beaver,
Walnut Creek, California

Preface

Virtually everyone I talk to wants a satisfying and fulfilling sex life—and this is particularly true of married couples. But is this goal being attained? I think that the answer is no. As a culture we may seem preoccupied with sex, given the media's emphasis on the way we look and perform, but what we see on television doesn't necessarily reflect what is really going on in our bedrooms.

A disparity still exists between what couples want and what they experience in their daily lives—hence their preoccupation with the subject of sex. When I first presented my agent with the idea for this book, he felt that a book about sex would be more marketable than one about marriage. Sex sells! It sells because we have a need for quality in our sex lives that is not being filled. We try to get this need met in all kinds of ways—through books, therapy, classes—anything that might help us in our quest for the magic key.

Why another book about sex? So far, I haven't seen a book that addresses the issue of sexuality in the context of a couple relationship in a way that the layperson can understand, and to which he or she can relate. True, the subject of sex in popular literature has been thoroughly dissected in books on female sexuality, male sexuality, orgasm, etc., but a person needs an entire library in order to look at the whole picture. One of my intentions in writing this book was therefore to offer a comprehensive package of information that deals with what really happens psychologically in a couple's sexual relationship. The issue as I see it is quality—the amount of pleasure, satisfaction, and fulfillment that people experience in their sex lives.

This book is a sequel to my previous book, *Beyond the Marriage Fantasy*. That book explores how a couple can have greater intimacy outside the bedroom—how they can intimately communicate with one another, and how they can resolve conflicts. It contains a chapter on sex, but much more is needed to do the subject justice.

In my counseling practice, before I look at a couple's sexual relationship, I make sure that their general relationship is sound, that their conflicts are resolved, and that they are able to talk to each other intimately. They need to be lovers outside the bedroom before they can experience a quality sexual relationship in the bedroom. I think that too often the subject of sex is taken out of the context of the whole relationship, and we forget that our sexuality is more than what we do in bed.

Some people ask, "Why should there have to be books, classes, and therapies devoted to sex in the first place? Isn't sex a natural function that doesn't require any learning or teaching? If left alone, won't nature take care of it on its own?" Many people are surprised to learn that the only thing natural (i.e., instinctual—that which doesn't require learning) about sex is the actual process of making babies, or reproduction. This aspect of sexuality in principle doesn't require a great deal of knowledge and intelligence. Ironically, this is really the only aspect of sexuality that we do learn about in our culture. By the time I graduated from high school, I knew how babies were made. But I didn't know how to enjoy making love to a woman. Everything I learned from parents, church, schools, and peers about pleasurable sexuality was in some way repressive; all the mixed messages, guilt trips, and fears that I inherited from these sources inhibited or repressed my so-called natural ability to enjoy the sexual experience. This suggests that sex might be a naturally pleasurable and fulfilling experience in this culture if we weren't taught all the dos and don'ts that inhibit us!

The emphasis of this book is on the aspect of sexuality that we are never taught—how to achieve maximum pleasure in our sexual lives and how to maintain that quality of pleasure over a long period of time. In our culture, this requires a type of sex education we never had.

The way we learn about the actual dynamics of sex between two people is through first-hand experience, which really means that we learn about sex through trial and error—unfortunately, mostly through error. Something so vitally important, so personal, and so sensitive as our sexual life we leave to fumbling around in the dark. Is it any wonder that we have so many hang-ups and fears about our sexual experience? And these feelings severely limit our ability to enjoy our full sexual potential.

Sex is a natural drive in all of us—like hunger and thirst—though unlike these latter drives, our sexuality can be repressed without fatal consequences. Everyone is a sexual person. Even those who seem to have no desire for sex have a potential to be very sexual. The challenge is to break through all the conditioning and inhibiting experiences that get in the way of enjoying our full sexual potential. It is my intention through this book to show how to break through the psychological traps to which we all may fall prey which get in the way of experiencing full sexual pleasure and fulfillment.

The main context for my discussion of sexuality will be that of the married couple, since marital sex is the most widely approved form of sexuality in our culture, since the majority of people marry, and also since most of my clinical experience has been gained from working with married couples. However, most of this material will also be relevant to the single person, the couple living together, or the gay couple.

One might think that since marriage is the most common context for sexual activity, marital sex must therefore be usually pleasurable and fulfilling. Yet just the contrary is true. Sex tends to occur less and less frequently through the course of a marriage. All around us we hear a constant outcry about the quality of sex in marriage and about the quality of marriage in general. Renowned sex therapists Masters and Johnson have suggested that half of all marriages involve some sexual dysfunction.

Any discussion of sexuality in this culture is bound to be emotionally charged. We are dealing with people's values of right and wrong, morality and immorality. My intent is to stay clear of moral issues. I respect everyone's values—who am I to judge? If a person's beliefs work, and the person is satisfied, then I have no objections. However, when a person's values, beliefs, and attitudes are not working and are interfering with their sexual life, then I can offer some alternatives. I can't tell you the right way to make love, but I can suggest some alternative ways of thinking and acting that may help you experience more sexual pleasure and fulfillment.

The material in this book has come from many sources, but the main source has been the many clients I have seen in my clinical practice as a sex therapist. These people have shared the most intimate aspect of their lives with me, enabling me to obtain both an education and a perspective available to few. Of course, I have received academic and professional training in the field of sexuality, but I have gained much more from clinical practice than from books. It is my hope that in sharing what I have learned from my clients with you through this book that I may help you too to enjoy more sexual satisfaction and fulfillment in your personal life.

Examples and references used in this book are based on actual situations I've encountered in counseling, but in some instances the cases described are composites of several actual cases and in all cases the names and details about each person have been changed.

—DANIEL BEAVER

Introduction

Over the past fifteen years I have addressed many groups on the subject of sexuality and relationships. Invariably, I'm asked how I became a sex therapist. How was it that I went into this specialty rather than more traditional forms of counseling and therapy?

My answer is always the same. It was not at all something I planned—perhaps fate played a big part in my choice. Certain doors opened up to me that I really wouldn't have known were there unless I had recognized the opportunity and walked through them.

I began my career in family therapy, taking a job with a family service agency soon after earning my master's degree in counseling. I had not been with the agency long when my supervisor took me aside and asked if I would consider attending a training class offered by the California Department of Public Health. It was entitled "Team Treatment to Couple Counseling."

The training program would be three months long, I was told, and I would get my full salary while attending, in addition to picking up some necessary professional training. I jumped at the chance, even before I'd explored what material was going to be covered.

To my own surprise and the surprise of my supervisor, the course turned out to be a Masters and Johnson sex therapy training. Over the next 90 days I received the first real sex education of my life, both from a personal and professional point of view.

My previous sex education was pretty limited. I had gotten the basic facts of reproduction (what a friend once referred to as "Birds and Bees 1-A") from my junior high gym coach. It consisted of one week of talks in a health and hygiene class. In high school, I had a follow-up course, this time taught by a young woman who was anything but comfortable talking about sex with a bunch of sweaty-palmed co-eds.

In my first year at college I became interested in looking at Masters and Johnson's new book, *The Human Sexual Response.*

9

However, when I went to the library I discovered it was kept locked in a glass cabinet. The librarian in charge of this cabinet was an elderly woman who guarded the books sequestered there as if they were top secret—delicate material not meant for the average library-goer. Whatever spirit had moved me to read this book was dampened by the prospect of having to pass muster with the keeper of the keys.

I took many psychology classes at the university, but there was only a single class offered on sexuality. It dealt with the sex life of beagles. While this might have been invaluable had I been interested in a career in veterinary medicine, I decided it wasn't for me.

It was from this grossly limited background in human sexuality that I entered the Masters and Johnson course. And it was here that I had to face the fact that I was only slightly more comfortable with the subject than that keeper of the keys in the college library. During the three-month course, I learned to use language and to talk about subjects that I had never before imagined. I had to work through some of my own misinformation about sex, and confront what was uncomfortable to me. Upon completion of the course, I had a brand new outlook not only about sexuality itself but about my own life and the meaning of having a long-term intimate relationship.

If this course awakened me to the role of sexuality in human relations, the next step in my sexual education helped open me physically. This phase of my learning was also more serendipitous than intentional. Back in the '70s, I often spoke at human sexuality courses given at the local colleges. On this particular occassion, the instructor had used up her budget for outside speakers, so in return for my presentation to her class she offered me a weekend massage class that she was teaching.

I agreed to make the trade, not giving too much thought to what it might involve. When I showed up for the class, however, it became quite clear that we were all going to be nude. I had never experienced anything like this in my life and I had all kinds of illusions run through my mind—not the least of which was that I would keep getting an erection. I was not alone in my discomfort. Others confessed to having similar concerns or being worried about how their bodies would compare to others'.

To my surprise, my exagerated sexual concerns quickly faded. For the most part, people in the group became quite comfortable with their nudity. We learned how to touch and be touched, to give and receive a therapeutic massage. Though sensuous and deeply nurturing, it was not a sexual experience. I left with new experience of the sensual nature of human life. Not only did this class open up new avenues of self-expression, pleasure, awareness, and communication in my own life, it provided me with new levels of understanding to share with my clients.

Over the years I have integrated with my professional knowledge a wide range of disciplines and skills associated with human sexuality. And like most therapists, I have allowed the lessons from my own life to enrich the lessons received by more formal routes. In this book, I have attempted to bring it all together in a form that is easily accessible for anyone wishing to deepen the enjoyment of sex and thus enrich those most intimate moments that we share with our lovers and mates.

Why You Are the Way You Are—
Sexual Attitudes, Beliefs, and Myths

Whenever I meet with a couple for the first time, we sit down and discuss their sexual history. From our discussions together, we begin to develop a sympathetic understanding of how their present ideas and feelings about sex and their own self-esteem have come about. In the beginning, many couples are skeptical about this process. To them, events that happened in the past are ancient history. However, after a sexual breakthrough or two, which allows them to experience deeper and more intimate levels of their relationship, they enthusiastically acknowledge the tremendous value of such work.

For each of us, our sexual history is both cultural and personal. What's the difference between the two? Admittedly, there are times when one laps over into the other. But in general, personal history is the sum of our sexual experiences, while cultural history is comprised of the sexual memories and beliefs of the human race. The latter are passed along to us through our parents, our peers, our art and literature, the media, and our institutions.

Surely one of the most important and powerful influences on human sexuality is religion. Because religion so thoroughly permeates the foundations of every modern society, this factor affects every one of us, whether we consider ourselves religious or not. For centuries, Judaism and Christianity have played major roles in defining what is acceptable sexual behavior in our society and what is not. When these religions developed thousands of years ago, their prime concerns were reproduction and the survival of the species. But there was one major difference between their respective teachings. Judaism taught that sex was something to be enjoyed in and of itself, but only within the context of marriage. Early Christian teachings, on the other hand, portrayed sex as inherently evil—though an evil vitally necessary for reproduction. Early Judeo-Christian teachings denigrated all sexual activity that did not directly lead to conception. Sexuality which was suspected of being carried out only for the pleasure of it—specifically masturbation, homosexuality, and extra- or premarital sex—was clearly not acceptable.

The views of these early cultures were clouded and enigmatic, since they expressed most of their teachings about sex through metaphor. These metaphors required interpretation, and they were subject to misinterpretation.

The Christian view of sexuality changed somewhat with the Protestant Reformation. Generally, the Protestants had a less negative attitude toward sexual matters than the Catholics. They didn't see sex as inherently sinful; neither did they regard chastity and celibacy as signs of virtue.

Sex and Religious Upbringing

Those of us who were brought up in a traditional religion were exposed to these teachings at a very vulnerable age. Whether they are right or wrong, they may still exert a great influence on us. The more orthodox or intense an individual's religious training during childhood, the greater the influence it will have on his or her sexual development and adult attitudes and feelings about sex. Even if an adult is no longer affiliated with his or her parents' religion, the effects of such exposure during childhood may still remain. Many of the clients that come to me for sex therapy are from families that were intensely Catholic, Baptist, or Jewish. While not everyone brought up in such a family has trouble with sex, a strong religious upbringing often plays a role in any difficulties that might occur in this area.

In the Renaissance period our cultural values and beliefs about sex underwent another shift. It was during this time that the concept of "pure love" developed among the upper classes. Pure love was seen as incompatible with the temptations of the flesh; therefore a distinction was made between love and sex, with sex having a lesser value. In some ways, this notion is still with us today.

In America, the Puritans added still another overlay on our sexual attitudes. It is a popular misconception that the Puritans were sexually repressive and inhibited. The reverse is actually true. They were surprisingly open and frank about sex. The Puritans were not anti-sexual in principle. They were vehemently against sexual activity outside the bonds of marriage. Their primary concern was with regulating behavior that threatened the stability of the family, such as adultery and illegitimate children. Puritan beliefs and teachings had a great influence on America's morals.

The Victorian age marked the next historical turning point in sexual thinking. Many of our present-day misconceptions have their roots in this period. Victorian sexual attitudes were primarily focused on women. Victorian England all but denied the existence of female sexuality. A decent woman was above sexual pleasure and only endured the sexual act as a duty to her husband—hence the common idea that sex is for the man and that it is the only thing he wants. The Victorian feminine ideal was angelic, innocent, and pure; woman was put on a pedestal and adored from afar.

A major difference between Victorian and Puritan attitudes was that the Puritans were only interested in sexual restriction outside marriage, whereas the Victorians wanted to control sexuality in all aspects of society, including within the institution of marriage.

One aspect of sexuality that obsessed the Victorians was the practice of masturbation. Many of today's myths about masturbation have their origins in this period. It was believed that masturbation causes insanity, headaches, epilepsy, hair on the palms, tuberculosis, and other ailments.

The main belief on which Victorian sexual ideology was based was that men have a limited supply of semen. It was believed that semen is a vital substance and that its spillage is a dangerous and potentially lethal waste. Victorian moralists wanted to repress, restrict, and inhibit the sexuality of an entire society so that it could be rechanneled to loftier ends.

The sexual attitudes of the Victorian period carried special significance, because they were advocated not just by the religious leaders of that time, but by the scientific and medical communities as well. At the turn of the nineteenth century, as society grew more urban and cosmopolitan, Victorian ideas began to appear unrealistic; the official code corresponded neither to the emotional nor the physical realities of the new technological society. The collapse of Victorian ideas was inevitable.

Sigmund Freud dealt a crippling blow to Victorian sexual philosophy with his theory that sexual repression was the cause of neurosis. By giving repression a bad name, Freud gave the free and open practice of sex a new legitimacy. By the time of World War I, the last vestiges of the Victorian period were fading. Yet many of its misconceptions lived on.

Weaving the Strands
Into the Thread of Today

All of the attitudes toward sex that we have been tracing seemed to coalesce and solidify in the 1950s. At that time, women's virginity was a major issue. Intercourse for women out of wedlock, or for just the pleasure of the moment, was condemned—a woman's reputation as being a "good girl" was at stake. The "bad girl" was one who involved herself in sexual intercourse without necessarily being in love or in a committed relationship.

For a woman to have intercourse with a man to whom she was not married was a symbolic act—it meant that she loved the man and assumed that he loved her and that they would get married at some point. Of course, many "had to" get married because of unforeseen pregnancies.

If the relationship ended soon after intercourse took place, or if the couple never got married, the woman could feel used by the man—he had "taken advantage" of her and she had lost her precious virginity. These concepts were not new to the 1950s, but took on a greater importance and emphasis during that time.

Men were immune from these restrictions because it was supposed that they needed to "sow their wild oats." The classic double standard prevailed. It held that casual sex was fine for men, but good girls shouldn't indulge unless they were in love.

In the 1960s, especially in the latter half of the decade, sexual values and behavior took a radical turn. At the time, it was called the "sexual revolution," though whether a real revolution actually occurred is still a question.

With the advent and subsequent popularity of the birth control pill, women were freed from the fear of pregnancy. Suddenly they had an entirely new level of sexual freedom—the freedom to have sex without fear of unwanted pregnancies. This freedom had an unexpected side effect: women felt more pressure to be involved sexually.

The pill released both men and women, but especially women, from the requirement that in order to engage in sex the couple needed to be married. As a result, sex was freed from the context of marriage. Almost immediately, it became a primary focus of advertising and media attention. As the commercialization of sex has advanced further and further into our private lives, the deeper and more personal meanings of sex have become increasingly obscured.

Has there been a sexual revolution? Have things really changed? From a technical point of view, yes. Women have a great deal more social freedom because of the pill. But the double standard still exists. Have basic attitudes changed? I don't think so. There is still a tremendous amount of ignorance and misinformation about sex.

In order for a revolution to be worthy of the name, it must struggle fiercely against the accepted values and customs of a society. By that standard, the sexual revolution died some time ago. As with every swing in our sexual history, there has been a counterswing towards sexual restriction. The new conservatism we're seeing emerge today hasn't just been produced by the ideologues of the Moral Majority; it has been hastened by the practical and real fears of sexually transmitted diseases (STD) and AIDS. Even the radical leaders of the sexual revolution seem to have returned to the old values of fidelity, devotion, stability, privacy, selectivity, and discretion.

Sources of Our Personal Sexual Conditioning

We have seen how our culture's attitudes toward sex were formulated. But how about us as individuals—how were our personal attitudes formed? How was information about sex communicated to us during our early years? The major sources were our parents, schools, religion, peers, and the media, as we've already noted. Each of these played an important role in shaping our sexual behaviors.

The first source was our parents. Many people believe that children should learn about sex in the home. And in reality, children do. But what they learn is too often not enough. Many parents, not knowing what to encourage and what to discourage, are overwhelmed by the idea of teaching their children about sex. Often parents say very little, or offer only the most basic facts—perhaps a brief discussion of the course of pregnancy.

Because no-one in the family talks about the subject much, the indirect message that the child receives is that there is something wrong about sex. When parents do give information, they are usually responding to specific questions the child brings up. The inquiry leads to uncertainty and discomfort for all involved. In the end, most of what parents teach their children about sex is communicated unconsciously. It isn't what our parents tell us about sex that matters; it is the way they deliver the message. And it is here that actions speak louder than words.

Our parents were our models. We based many of our sexual attitudes on what we observed. How did they touch each other? How much time did they spend alone together? How did they express their love for one another? These are the things that shaped our sexual consciousness. The real key was our emotional reaction to what our parents modeled. Were we comfortable, disgusted, or afraid? These emotional reactions created and reinforced the sexual attitudes that are still with us today.

Our parents did the best that they could, given their backgrounds, though some do better than others in establishing healthy sexual attitudes in their children. But even if they did a lousy job in this department, it serves no purpose to blame them. As you'll see in this book, you have the power to rewrite your life script and not feel victimized by your past—if you really want to change.

Couples who work through the conflicts of their own sexual history, inevitably ask, "How can I avoid passing on to my children the same sexual hangups I received as a kid?" The answer is to make sure that you are comfortable with your own sexuality. If you are not, you will transmit your discomfort to your children and it will stay with them into adult life. If you, as a parent, know you are not comfortable with the subject of sex, then find a trusted person who is, and let your children receive sexual information from that person.

Sex Information and Schools

Sometimes our sexual history involves the schools. Many parents have looked to the schools to provide sex education for their children, because of their own discomfort with the subject. This approach is fraught with controversy. Some parents are bitterly opposed to sex education for a variety of reasons. In this difficult climate, sex education in the schools has come a long way in the past twenty years, but still falls short of what is really needed. Living in fear of community pressure groups, the schools try their best to present needed information.

Historically, the treatment of sex education in schools has focused primarily on biology and reproduction. In California, the first subject addressed is menstruation. At some point during the sixth grade, boys and girls are separated, and the girls are shown a movie on the subject. The boys are, of course, very curious, and there is a lot of giggling all around.

It is in junior high school that the subject of sex first appears in the curriculum. My first sex education class came in the eighth grade, and the teacher was my gym coach. We took two weeks out of our regular gym schedule to learn about sex, drugs, and venereal disease—not necessarily in that order. The class covered the basic anatomy and physiology of reproduction; there was no discussion about how the sperm got to the egg. That was left to our imagination, and the coach probably didn't want to touch that subject. The context seems crazy and funny to me looking back—a macho gym coach teaching such a delicate subject in an environment of tension and unease. Sex was juxtaposed with drugs and venereal disease, two of society's evils. The unspoken message was that they fell into the same category.

For most students, the next exposure to the subject of sex was in high school, in either biology or health classes. But again, the emphasis was on the biological and physiological aspects of reproductive sex. There is nothing wrong with studying this material. The problem is that the discussion was very limited, ignoring the emotional and pleasurable aspects of sex. Perhaps these were too controversial for school. But as a result, we too often learned about the pleasurable side of sex only in the back seat of a car or from the stories of other kids in the locker room.

The Influence of Religion

Invariably, my early discussions with couples come around to the subject of how the beliefs of their churches impact on their sexuality. Some religious organizations, usually the more conservative or orthodox religions, are very direct about specific sexual dos and don'ts. Other times, the sexual messages are indirect and left to individual interpretation. This creates problems, because a young person, having very little knowledge or experience about sex, is unable to check out his or her interpretations with reality. As a consequence, many false assumptions and myths have developed about sex. These beliefs stay with us into adulthood, negatively affecting our sexual behavior. Even if a person is no longer affiliated with the religion in which he was raised, the sexual attitudes and beliefs learned at that time may still remain.

The major problem with the sexual information disseminated by religious organizations is that it tends to be slanted to their belief system. It is not presented objectively. Generally speaking, religions emphasize control and repression of sex outside the bond of marriage.

One problem created by the limitation of sexuality to the marriage relationship is that it puts people in a double bind—they're damned if they do and damned if they don't.

Those who are damned if they don't are the many women I see who put their sexuality on hold until the right man comes along for them to marry. They may wait for years. Then, once they are married, suddenly it's okay to be sexual and they are expected to turn their sexual feelings on as if they were wired to a light switch. Unfortunately, human beings aren't put together like electronic devices. Most of us find it virtually impossible to suddenly respond sexually when we've been repressing such feelings for a long time. Even though we suddenly have permission to be sexual, the old "you shouldn't" tapes are still grinding away in the background. As a result, we feel guilty, which gets in the way of enjoying this area of human experience.

This double bind can apply equally to women and men. Usually we receive the double message that it's not really okay to be sexual before marriage, but "boys will be boys." You might assume that the incidence of teenage sex argues that the taboo against premarital sex has disappeared, but this is simply not true in my experience. While the sexual activity level of teenagers is high, cultural attitudes and beliefs still don't support this behavior. This leads me to wonder if such early activity isn't the expression of rebellion rather than sexuality.

Another historical factor that influenced the development of our sexuality was our peer group. Since our parents, schools, and churches were unable to offer clear, accurate, and unbiased sexual information that went beyond the basic reproductive facts, an information vacuum was created. Generally, it was our peer group that filled this vacuum.

The trouble is that peer groups tend to perpetuate all the myths about sex that have been handed down from previous generations. All the falsehoods about masturbation (for instance the idea that you will grow hair on your palms if you masturbate) are still being passed along today in junior high school. To complicate matters, when we started learning about sex from our peers we were thirsty for any sexual information we could obtain to help explain all the changes we were feeling in our bodies. Not having an authoritative base of sex information to compare with what we learned in the street, we accepted the street information.

We learned unhealthy emotional attitudes along with the misinformation. Particularly with young men, discussions about sex tend to bring out attitudes of competition and one-upmanship. A boy may pretend that he knows all about sex so that his friends will think he is experienced with girls. Playing this game of pretend keeps him in a constant state of ignorance and anxiety.

Children whose primary source of sex information is their peers are frequently exposed to pornography. *Playboy, Penthouse* and other even more graphic magazines are the sex textbooks of the locker room and street. When light or hard-core pornography becomes an individual's source of information, the subject is seen out of its only healthy and meaningful context—an intimate relationship. The person becomes handicapped in the vital skill of being a lover in a long-term relationship. He or she never learns to connect what happens outside the bedroom with the more physical aspects of the relationship.

So our peer groups have a tremendous impact on shaping our sexual attitudes. We found answers to questions that our church, school, and parents were afraid to answer—that is, if we had the courage to ask. The only problem was that many of the answers we got were wrong or distorted. For a teenager, learning about sex is like putting together a large jigsaw puzzle without a map or rules to go by. We grasp one piece from a friend, another from a sex education class, a bit from an overheard conversation in a locker room. Our chances of assembling an accurate picture from these fragments is slim.

Media Messages

The last major source of sex information and one which is an increasingly important part of our sexual history, is the media. The sexual messages we receive from television, radio, music lyrics, motion pictures, books, and magazines are both overt and subliminal. The subliminal messages are very powerful, since we are learning without realizing it and therefore can't question or resist the information we're taking in. Advertisers capitalize on subliminal communication to sell their products. Just as we may find ourselves whistling jingles for products, or reaching for a product in the grocery store that we have never tried before and don't really want, we may find ourselves expressing sexual attitudes that have bombarded us through the media.

The communications from the various forms of media are so powerful that they have increased the speed of the sexual learning process. Just from watching television, a thirteen-year-old's superficial knowledge about sex increases dramatically. Many people complain that children are too quickly losing their innocence. If we operate from the assumption that sexual behavior is learned through experience rather than instinct, then the greatest sex educator has been Hollywood, by way of movies and television.

What are the sexual messages that television and the movies convey? In the past twenty years television has changed greatly in its handling of sex, but one thing has remained constant: it always creates fantasies of how life is being lived—whether it's "Father Knows Best," where family problems are solved to everyone's complete satisfaction in minutes, or "Dallas," where conflicts are solved through deceit and violence.

Programs like these expose viewers to a reality completely different from everyday experience—a perfectly presented fantasy. Many prime time shows give the impression that extramarital affairs and divorce are just a normal part of life. When adults, and especially when vulnerable teenagers, are constantly exposed to these images, they tend to forget that what they are watching is fantasy. They start comparing their own experience with what they see, and their own personal lives seem dull by comparison. In conjunction with the programs themselves, commercial sponsors communicate their own sexual messages.

Of course, television is not the only commercial medium that uses sexuality in advertising. You can see and hear the hype everywhere—on billboards, in magazines, and on the radio, selling everything from power tools to jeans. Along with the product that is being promoted there is always a beautiful man or woman—and an unmistakable innuendo. And ever since women's sexual emancipation began, advertisers have been treating the public to a slow striptease, as the bras get skimpier and the bikini bottoms fade to little more than a string.

The problem with this sexual sales pitch is that we are again set up with the fantasy of the perfect sex partner. This fantasy is forced upon both men and women by a media bombardment that uses images of sex goddesses, beauty queens, and "hunks" to sell product.

The woman in the ad does the selling by exciting men sexually while giving them no gratification. The suggestion is that we get a piece of her by buying the product. This is all going on at a sub-conscious level, so that we aren't even consciously aware of what is taking place. The message the man is receiving is that his sexuality is defined in terms of products or things. Cars, hair styles, colognes, motorcycles, toothpaste—these are the things that will make him sexually irresistible. So what happens when he purchases all these things and the pretty girl doesn't materialize? Frustration and disappointment set in, with an accompanying sense of sexual inadequacy. With this kind of programming, it's not surprising that men tend to express their feelings of love by the giving of material objects.

The message from the media to women is similar. Through the image of the sex goddess, women are shown what they have to be like—and what they must buy—in order to be considered sexually desirable in our culture. Television commercials in particular offer no middle ground, just extremes—the sex goddess on one end, and the housewife worried about the stains in her sink on the other. The reality for women is the same as for men: they can never live up to the Madison Avenue image no matter how many things they buy. As a result, many women don't feel good about their body image, and this affects their sexuality and general self-esteem.

The information and role-modeling we get from media sources are a departure from reality. We, as a culture, are being set up for frustration and a great amount of dissatisfaction because we tend to compare our own personal realities with the fantasies portrayed by the media. Recently, television has been trying to cover controversial issues such as homosexuality, abortion, and incest in a more realistic way. But as long as commercials make these shows possible, distorted images of sexual perfection will continue to proliferate and continue to be a part of our sexual consciousness.

Choosing to Let Go of the Past

Now that we have an understanding of the foundations for our sexual histories, and in turn for our sexual beliefs and attitudes, the question arises: How can we change our thinking to free us from our sexual hangups? Much of the practice of sex therapy revolves around this question. Many people see the need to change, but are held back from doing so because of their past sexual development. Past sexual experience can be broken down into two basic components: second-hand information from the sources described above, or first-hand experience from our own lives, along with the thoughts and emotions associated with such experience.

Unleashing the Natural Child Within

A very useful tool for helping us change our sexual beliefs and attitudes is the Transactional Analysis (TA) model of internal communication. This model describes our inner dialogue—the way we talk to ourselves—in terms of three basic modes (Fig. 1).

Every adult has each of the three modes active at one time or another in his or her consciousness. The first mode is called the parent. It is the parent part of us that embodies many of the beliefs and attitudes we've described in our discussion of our sexual histories. The parent has two parts: the critical parent and the nurturing parent. The critical parent developed as we were growing up. It was as if our minds were a clean slate of wax and all the authority figures in our life—our parents, teachers, and ministers—etched into our slate with a hot knife what was right or wrong, good or bad, what we should or should not do. Being children, we took this information in as if it were gospel, never questioning its validity—if they said it was true, then it was.

Figure 1

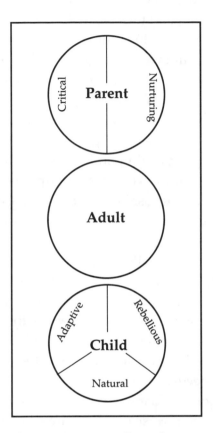

Another part of our parent mode is the nurturing aspect. The nurturing parent is best described by thinking of all the qualities that we would associate with a nurturing individual—someone who is supportive, understanding, accepting, concerned, ministering, and caring. While we often think of our past histories as having only a negative influence, it is here that we also embody positive influences of our pasts.

The second mode of thinking and behaving is the adult. We could label this aspect "the computer." This is the part of us that takes in information from our environment, evaluates the information, makes decisions, and takes action based on these decisions. We are in the adult mode when buying a car: we look for the best price, we consider whether the payments are affordable, we compare different features, and then we make our decision.

While the adult can include information from both parent and child, its primary focus is how things feel (emotionally) in the present. When it looks at past history, it weighs its information against more objective facts.

The last mode of communication is the child. Like the parent, the child has more than one part. The part we habitually express as a child depends a great deal upon how we related to our parents and other adults when we were growing up. There are three parts of the child that are most useful to consider in our discussion: (1) the adaptive child; (2) the rebellious child; and (3) the natural child.

The adaptive child usually does what his or her parents want. This child lives up to the expectations of authority figures in order to receive praise, acceptance, and love. If this mode of behavior and thinking is dominant when we grow up, the result is a loss of identity. The person becomes a chameleon, adapting to the spouse or companion's needs and wishes instead of expressing his or her own feelings and needs.

The opposite of the adaptive child is the rebellious child. This sort of child does the reverse of what parents and teachers expect. The payoff for this type of behavior is the attention the child receives. Although the attention is negative, it is still attention. The "class clown" is a rebellious child who gets into trouble with his or her teachers and parents, but gets a lot of attention from them, as well as from peers.

The last part, the natural child, is the one most relevant to the subject of this book, for it is here that the origins of our sexuality are discovered. The natural child is the two-year-old in each of us. When we were two years old we felt and expressed all our emotions; there was no emotional censorship or repression. In a sense, we experienced all the emotions available to us at that time— anger, joy, sadness, pleasure, and pain. We could act spontaneously and be totally uninhibited, and we didn't worry about what others thought.

All of these characteristics are vital to a healthy sexual experience. Unfortunately, the natural child component in our psychological makeup gets bombarded with negative messages from our parents, peers, and society, and is often repressed as a result. It can be bruised and battered by its history. For some of us, it is only when we become intoxicated that the natural child is able to come out of hiding.

Many people don't feel that they are capable of experiencing sexual pleasure and fulfillment. But since this natural child exists in all of us, regardless of the sexual history that has driven it into hiding, I believe that everyone has the potential to enjoy and receive sexual fulfillment. Generally, the only problem with sexually inhibited people is the psychological programming they received while growing up—the history that restrains their natural child from expressing itself sexually. The key to releasing their sexuality is the reprogramming of all the old messages from the past, literally rewriting one's history. We do this by dialoguing with our inner parent, adult, and child.

Dialoguing with these parts of us is far easier than it sounds. When you are feeling stuck or troubled, or if you simply have questions about a feeling you are having, remind yourself of these parts within you. Pretend that you are actually able to talk with each of the parts, asking questions and listening for answers. Or, you can simply ask yourself, What are the beliefs that my parent holds? What things does it warn or scold me about that get in my way of enjoying sex more?

Meanwhile, feed your adult new information, through books such as this one. When your parent starts nagging you with its list of shoulds and shouldn'ts let your adult step in to correct faulty perceptions or fill in voids in your parent's understanding.

Embrace your natural child. Assure yourself that the feelings you have which originate here are healthy. Let your adult acknowledge this part of your child and seek appropriate ways for its expressions to unfold.

As you get to know these different aspects of yourself better and better, you begin to develop a wider range of choices about your sexuality. Your emotions cease to be quite the confusing mystery they once were and you see that it is possible to make choices about them.

Reshaping Our Inner Dialogue

The parent, adult, and child form the basic idea of the Transactional Analysis model. How do these internal voices communicate? The most common and destructive messages we give ourselves are those that originate from the critical parent within us. These are messages like, "I should," "I shouldn't," "I ought to," or self put-downs like "I'm stupid," "I'm dumb," "I'm lazy," or "I'm irresponsible." If someone spoke to you like that you would probably feel resentful. We feel the same resentment internally when we talk to ourselves this way. The child within us reacts with anger, and the way we expressed that emotion with our own parents will largely determine how we express it as an adult.

Some people express their anger by displacing it onto someone or something close by, like a spouse, child, or pet. Others may repress the anger and become depressed. People with active internal critical parents also tend to have low self-esteem. Those who tended to be rebellious as children will also rebel against their own critical parent (Fig. 2).

So how does all of this relate to sex? Understanding this psychological dynamic is important in freeing our natural child so that we can choose to define and express our sexuality, no longer dominated by the programming of our past history, which finds its voice in the critical parent. This liberation from undesirable aspects of our history begins when we learn to gain access to the adult within us.

The adult in us expresses itself through the phrases, "I want," or "I don't want." How does an adult know what he or she wants,

Figure 2

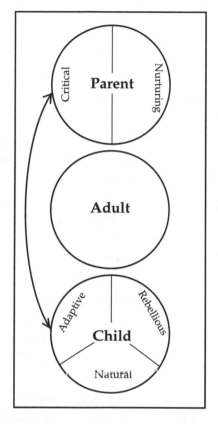

"I shouldn't"
"I've got to"
"I have to"

Critical **Parent** Nurturing

Adult

Adaptive **Child** Rebellious

Natural

Equals:

Anger
Depression
Low self-esteem
Rebellion

and what makes the choice right for him or her? We do this by getting in touch with feelings. Sometimes clients ask questions such as, "Should I sleep with him on the first date?" "Should I leave my wife?" or "Should I get married?"—as if the answers to these questions can only be found outside themselves, by others who they consider to be authorities. Seeing the therapist as the authority in such matters, they want me to tell them how they should run their life. They look to me as the parent.

The only answers any of us can hope to live with are those which come when we ask ourselves how we feel. Am I comfortable with the idea of sleeping with him on our first date? If not, then why do it? When people ignore or override their own feelings, they usually regret it later. If you are emotionally torn, then it's best not to make a choice or take action until the emotional conflict has been resolved.

We acquire most of our sexual beliefs and attitudes as children. But when we reach adulthood, many of us feel the need to shed those beliefs and attitudes. We can only do so by rewriting the rules that we received and assembled in our minds as children. If we say that we don't agree with what was said back then by parent figures, yet fail to replace their teachings with new beliefs and attitudes, we leave a vacuum. Usually the old beliefs and attitudes will creep back in to fill the vacuum.

As an example, consider the history of a woman who has been married for twelve years, has a couple of children, but hasn't really been able to enjoy sex with her husband. When she was thirteen, her mother gave her the message, directly or indirectly, that she shouldn't be sexual. Her mother told her this because she was concerned about her daughter's welfare, not because she wanted her daughter to be sexually inhibited. She was concerned about her daughter losing her virginity, becoming pregnant, or contracting a sexually transmitted disease, all of which are legitimate concerns with regard to adolescent sexuality.

Now the daughter is an adult and married and finds that the old attitudes—which perhaps should be ancient history but aren't—are getting in the way of fully enjoying her sexuality. She feels guilty about sex because she hasn't given herself permission as an adult to be sexual. She hasn't rewritten the rules to make it acceptable for her to enjoy her sexual feelings. After a while, her guilt may start to feel natural, as if it has always been a part of her sexual makeup. But she wasn't born feeling guilty and she needn't live with guilt now.

The process of examining our sexual history, identifying the rules that guide us, and then making choices about keeping or changing those rules, is not always easy. But breaking with obsolete rules is a key to becoming an adult.

Is Change Possible?

Now we understand some of the historical events that shaped our sexual attitudes and behavior. But the question remains, How does an individual go about changing them? Some experts believe that our attitudes must change before our behavior will. Others argue the contrary. In my experience I find that change is most complete, lasting, and rewarding when we deal with both attitude and behavior simultaneously.

To the extent that it's possible within the restrictions of a book, I have combined the two approaches. Of course, any book can only expand awareness and offer new insights and choices. What happens with that new awareness is up to the reader. Whether or not it gets translated into new behavior is never within the author's power. And it is only in this translation from insight to action that real change can even occur.

Meat and Potatoes Sex—
The Tender Trap

Often I find that a couple's sexual difficulties are much simpler than they might have feared, being traced to the fact that they tend to make love in a repetitive pattern. The irony is that they often continue this pattern even though both are unhappy with it. They keep going down the same street in the hope that somehow something magic will happen to make their sexual experience different. They keep following the same pattern, not because they like it, but because they simply don't know what else to do.

One of our most commonly held cultural beliefs is that sex is natural and that good sex is instinctive. It is comforting to believe that if people just keep working at their sexual relationship it will improve; that nature will take care of the problem over time. Unfortunately, the contrary is true. The longer a couple keeps following the same sexual pattern, the more likely they are to escalate any problems they may be having.

Even if they are aware of no problems, a couple may follow the same sexual behavioral pattern because they are afraid to change. It becomes emotionally risky for them to leave the beaten path.

36 • *More Than Just Sex*

Heading into Unfamiliar Territory

I have know many people who got stuck in a sexual routine because they were unable to communicate with their partners about the changes they would like to make. Usually in the beginning of a couple's sexual relationship, they feel no pressing need to communicate specific sexual wants and needs, since the novelty of being together intimately is sufficiently exciting and stimulating in itself. Once they have passed this phase, communication becomes increasingly important.

Most of us who have grown up in this culture find it difficult to talk openly and honestly about sex. So it should come as no surprise that we don't talk about our sexual wants when we first become aware of them. The very idea of such a discussion brings up all kinds of fears and anxieties—not the least of which is the possibility of being judged by the other person.

Even if one person in the relationship is able to break through his or her inhibitions and communicate, this is not enough. There needs to be mutual openness between the partners for their relationship to work. Let's say, for example, that your partner begins communicating openly about his sexual needs before you are ready to do the same. You might then feel that he is putting pressure on you, a pressure that might make you feel like retreating further into your shell; on the other hand, his greater openness might signal you that it's safe and acceptable to talk about sexual matters, encouraging you to open up, too.

When you can't communicate with your partner, you tend to stay stuck in the same "safe" sexual pattern that you established at the beginning of your relationship. While it may have been fun when you first got together, in time it becomes a boring routine, a pattern that neither one enjoys. As the excitement diminishes, so does your desire, and thus the frequency of sex diminishes, too.

Sex doesn't become boring simply because you're married. Yet, all too many married couples assume it's inevitable and give up on having an exciting sex life. Others still want excitement, and assume that the best way to achieve it is to have other lovers. In some cases, for one member of a couple to acquire a new lover can bring needed change to the sexual patterns in the established relationship, but usually not without creating more problems than anyone bargained for.

Sex is like dancing—if you can't teach your partner new steps, or say when your toe is being stepped on, you will quickly tire of the same old tune. You'll either stop dancing with that person or start looking for a new partners.

Because of their individual personalities, some people seek structure and sameness in their lives. Familiarity and predictability gives them a sense of security. Even while the predictable pattern may give them a sense of security, it can also cause them to feel bored. If you are such a person, you might feel caught in a double bind, wanting your sex life to be more exciting but also wanting the predictable structure that "doing the same old thing" provides.

Leaving behind the security of the structure means taking a risk, and it means becoming more emotionally vulnerable to your partner. The risk usually entails the fear of rejection or judgment for doing something different. Therefore, one basic requirement for improving a sexual relationship is the development of a high level of trust between the partners, a subject we'll be exploring in greater depth in chapter three.

Prescription for Change

All change requires three things: Awareness, Motivation, and Acceptance.

Awareness.

You need to be aware that there are alternative attitudes and behavior patterns that you can choose, in addition to those you already know. Without the awareness of new possibilities, you are stuck with myths and ignorance. This awareness is particularly helpful when you find yourself stuck in an unsatisfying routine—

which is almost always the case when a couple or individual is experiencing sexual difficulties.

As important as awareness is to the process of change, it does not produce change by itself. Having intellectual insight into the reasons for your present behavior, or knowledge of alternatives, may make you wiser. But to break the inertia of long-standing habits you need more than insight and knowledge—you need a strong emotional desire for change. This brings us to the subject of motivation.

Motivation.

To take intellectual awareness and put it into action, you must have motivation. Even though you may have an awareness of what you could do to improve you sex life, it doesn't necessarily follow that you will change unless you are motivated.

So what motivates people? From my clinical experience, what motivates people is emotion, not logic or rationality. Does it hurt enough? Are you frustrated enough, or scared, or angry enough to change your behavior?

Of course, the quantity of hurt, frustration, fear, or anger required to shift people varies from one person to another. Every-one has a different tolerance for emotional discomfort. I find that men usually have less hesitation about seeking help for personal sexual frustration than they have about seeking help for general marital problems. For women, the reverse is true.

Acceptance.

The third requirement for sexual change is acceptance. Of the three elements, this may be the most important. Acceptance implies the absence of judgment. If you are made to feel you are wrong, you will resist change. To change, you must feel that the way you are now is accepted. This does not mean that you will stay the same, or that you have to like the way you are now. Acceptance simply means being patient and caring of the situation just as it is. It's a given. It's where you have to begin.

Until recently, men have tended to judge women sexually, telling them how they should or should not be. Not until the advent of the women's liberation movement did women begin to define their own sexuality apart from men's judgment.

Within a relationship, sexual judgment can be deadly to development and growth. Sexual change does not take place in an atmosphere of judgment. Instead, judgment usually produces resistance to change on the part of the person feeling judged. I often hear statements like, "If you were a real man, you would…" Or "The other women I've been to bed with always liked it when I…." Or "What's wrong with you? Other women don't take so long reaching orgasm." Or "The other men I've been with didn't have to be told what to do."

These statements, and others like them, are made with the intent of changing the other person's sexual behavior. Usually, however, they produce resentment and anger, and lead to defensiveness, rebellion, and resistance to change. The bottom line is really quite simply stated: While judgment is intended to produce change, it generally has the opposite effect.

Embracing the Desire to Change

While you and your partner may be very motivated to change, you probably don't know how to get out of the rut in which you find yourselves. If you did, you obviously wouldn't have any problem. Whatever else you do at this point, it is vital that you stop judging and blaming each other. As a young woman once told me after she and her husband had succeeded in achieving a new level of intimacy in their relationship, "It took both of us to get off the track, and it took both of us to get back on."

Some Ruts Are Deeper Than Others

Many couples who come for help have a history of unpleasant or mediocre sexual experiences, that over time have worsened rather than improved. If they keep following the same sexual pattern, the results are sadly predictable. But when a couple receives new information or insight about how they might behave sexually—whether from a book, a class, or from therapy—they won't know the effect on their relationship until they start using their new information.

It is essential that each partner gives the other the opportunity to change, and it is important that they do so without predicting what the other's sexual behavior will be. Statements like, "Every time I try to initiate sex she always refuses," and "Whenever I tell him what would make me feel better sexually, he withdraws and feels attacked," project old behavior into the future, and such behavior-forecasting sabotages change. If one or both partners has new information regarding behavioral or attitudinal change, they need to be given the chance to put that new information to use. Not only is it essential that each gives the other the opportunity to change, but that each gives him- or herself the same opportunity as well.

It doesn't matter how old a person is, or how long he or she has been in a sexual relationship. That person can change if he or she is sufficiently motivated and knows how. When someone says, "This is who I am and if you don't like what you see, then you might as well leave, because I'm not changing," that person is acting as if his or her behavior and thinking are somehow genetic. This kind of love-it-or-leave-it attitude obviously blocks personal growth. What the person is really saying is, "I don't want to change." They are choosing not to change; it's not that they can't, it's that they won't. So, give yourself a chance to change—if you dare to take the risk, you might pleasantly surprise yourself!

The Most Common Rut

Over my years of counseling, I've noticed one particular pattern that keeps occurring among my clients, most of whom are white, middle- to upper-class suburban couples.

Generally speaking, the husband is the one who initiates sexual activity most often—typically in the evening after the children have gone to sleep. He waits until they are is in the bedroom and their television viewing is over for the evening. There probably hasn't been much, if any, intimate communication between them prior to going to bed. Also, one or both may be physically tired from the day's activities.

When they get into bed, the husband initiates sex by touching his wife's breasts and genitals with very little general body touching. His touching is very goal-oriented, his main purpose in touching his partner is to get her aroused enough to have intercourse.

Feeling the pressure to have sex with her husband whether she wants to or not, the wife consents to his overtures. She may feel that it is less hassle to just get it over with so that she can get him off her back (at least figuratively) for that evening.

Once the husband has touched his wife for what he considers a sufficient period of time, he initiates intercourse. Usually, he seems to be in a hurry. He senses his wife's "Hurry up and get it over with" attitude, so he isn't likely to prolong the experience. Also, he himself may be in a hurry because he knows that he has to get up early in the morning and go to work. The emotional atmosphere between the couple is tense, rather than playful or passionate.

Once intercourse occurs, usually with the husband in the "missionary position," he ejaculates fairly quickly; this happens because of the anxiety and tension between the partners. Once he ejaculates, he gives his wife a kiss, they hug each other, they roll over, and go to sleep.

The husband's sexual tension has been relieved. His wife may have experienced some physical closeness, but that's about all. For her, there hasn't been much pleasure in this experience. It shouldn't be too surprising, then, that the woman in this relationship is not very motivated to initiate sexual activity. While she may occasionally initiate sex out of guilt, feeling that it's her wifely duty to make sure that she satisfies her husband's sexual needs, at the same time she may also feel sexually inadequate because she isn't as sexually motivated to be with her husband as he is with her.

"What's wrong with me? Why don't I want to make love to him?" she may ask herself.

The sexual pattern described here is a stereotype, of course. Obviously, everyone doesn't make love this way. But perhaps you found that some parts of this description seem familiar. If you did, you're probably wondering what you can do to get out of this rut. As we'll see in the next chapter, the key lies in paying attention to our emotions.

Intimate Connection—
The Ultimate Aphrodisiac

Before there can be mutually pleasurable and deeply satisfying physical intimacy, there must be a groundwork of emotional intimacy. Without emotional intimacy, the quality of any sexual relationship will diminish over time. But what enables emotional intimacy to develop and flourish?

Often when a couple comes to see me, they talk about the lack of good sex in their relationship. Usually this means low frequency and little pleasure. They seem like roommates who occasionally have sex together. They have stopped being lovers outside the bedroom—and, in essence, they've stopped in the bedroom as well. There is virtually no constructive verbal expression of emotions between them.

There is a difference between loving someone and being "in love" with someone. From what I've seen, when you are in love with a person, you are emotionally involved. There is no emotional censorship to block the communication of feelings. It is this free flow of emotional expression that keeps a couple's relationship alive and vital. The one key to maintaining a pleasurable, long-term sexual relationship is to make sure that this "emotional bloodline" is never severed.

Blocks to Emotional Expression

Unfortunately, there are certain attitudes or beliefs common in our culture that tend to block emotional expression. One is the attitude that tends to invalidate a lover's emotions. It might be expressed in statements like these:

"Oh, Jane, you shouldn't get so upset over such a little thing."

"You're not being very rational or logical to feel the way you do."

"You're just being too emotional."

The person making these statements—let's call him Dick—is essentially saying that Jane shouldn't be experiencing the emotions that she is, in fact, experiencing. Naturally, she feels hurt and angry. If I were to ask her if she is now going to continue to express how she feels emotionally to her lover, assuming he continues to invalidate her feelings in this way, she would probably respond with a resounding "No!" Right at that point, Dick and Jane go from being lovers to being roommates, because Jane is removing herself emotionally from the relationship. (Of course, this can go both ways; if Jane were making similar statements to Dick, he undoubtedly would turn off to her emotionally.)

When Dick and Jane go to bed that night, and Dick makes sexual advances, Jane responds by saying that she's not in the mood.

She says, "I don't feel close to you, so it's difficult to make love to you."

Dick seems confused. "Well, let's make love; then you will feel close to me."

Too late, Dick!

Another common way we block emotional flow is when we judge certain emotions, thinking that some emotions—such as anger, hurt, frustration, jealousy, and fear—are negative or bad, and are therefore ones we shouldn't express. But what is a person to do with these feelings? What we usually do is to bury or repress them in the hope that they will simply go away. But emotions do not go away just because we want them to or because we ignore them. We may not be aware of the emotion after a while, but it is still there. Don't fool yourself. The feeling is "underground" in the subconscious, being expressed in all sorts of ways through moods and behavior—in ways we may not even realize. Sometimes the repressed emotions remain subliminal for a long time until something happens to bring them to consciousness.

Often these unexpressed emotions can inhibit our sexual desire or interest. There is a common attitude that reinforces our tendency to judge emotions; I remember learning it from my grandmother, who used to tell me, "Don't say anything unless you have something nice or positive to say."

If I follow my grandmother's advice, I can't tell my wife which things she does that makes me angry, frustrated, or hurt; I can only tell her how I love her and feel attracted to her. This may seem like a good idea at first, but the reality is that if I can't express to her my so-called negative feelings, over a period of time I won't be able to express any of my feelings. The relationship will become emotionally dead, and our sex life will become mechanical and boring.

At Thanksgiving and Christmas, when family members are gathered together to celebrate, my grandmother's advice might well apply. Then we are with relatives we may only see once a year. However, if taken to heart with someone you love, the only-express-positive-feelings theory can be disastrous.

By holding back or censoring emotions, we burn up a great deal of physical energy—just how much depends on how much emotion we are sitting on or holding back. When we do this, we lose our sexual energy, or sexual drive. To make sure that the emotional bloodlines in your relationship keep flowing, accept that whatever your lover feels emotionally is a fact for him or her. Never invalidate those emotions, even if they make no sense to you, or you don't feel the same way; it doesn't matter—that's how they feel.

Like it or not everyone has their own emotional reality. To accept it does not mean you agree with it; more importantly, it means that you respect that person's right to have an emotional life different than yours.

If you want your lover to stay intimately close and turned on to you sexually, you need to accept how that person feels; otherwise, it's as if you were taking a knife and cutting the arteries of your relationship and letting it slowly bleed to death.

Vulnerability

In any relationship, the key to intimacy is vulnerability. Vulnerability is the degree to which a person shares information about him or herself that leaves open the possibility of being hurt. Vulnerability is relinquishing control. If we cannot give up control, intimacy is impossible.

Vulnerability is essential to both verbal and sexual communication. In other words, we must experience vulnerability both inside and outside the bedroom. There must first be emotional vulnerability if there is going to be willing physical vulnerability.

Vulnerability at the verbal level involves the expression of emotions through words. Telling your lover what you are experiencing emotionally puts you in a vulnerable position; you are letting your partner know you in a way that perhaps few people do. As a result, your lover doesn't have to guess or read your body language. You are not telling your lover what you think about him or her, but instead how you feel inside. You are giving a very special gift by sharing this information (no matter what the emotions are that you are sharing) because you are opening yourself to possible judgment or rejection.

If your lover responds in the same way by sharing his or her emotions, then you have created intimacy. If this is your usual experience, yours is an intimate relationship. If your lover responds by judging your feelings or withholding her or his own, then the two of you have some work to do together, if intimacy is your goal. But if you are afraid to take the risk of expressing your emotions because you think you might get hurt, then you are not giving intimacy a chance to grow, and the relationship will probably never become intimate.

Of course, sexual satisfaction doesn't always require a high degree of vulnerability and emotional sharing; there is usually little of either in the case of the one-night stand, or in the beginning of a new relationship. In these situations, sexual pleasure is fueled by newness and the sense of the unknown. Once the novelty wears off, however, the couple must decide if they want to become more involved with each other by becoming vulnerable. If they don't open up to each other emotionally, yet keep seeing each other sexually, their relationship will probably lose its zest.

Over time, the more two people are able to communicate their vulnerabilities verbally, the greater their ability to be vulnerable in the physical/sexual aspect of their relationship as well.

Wants and Needs

Being vulnerable verbally requires expressing your wants and needs to your partner. When you name something you want, you are exposing yourself to possible disappointment. If I tell my wife that I want to spend Friday night with her and she says she has other plans, I'm going to feel disappointed; some people would even take this as rejection. If my wife responds positively, we'll have a good time. It's not knowing the response beforehand that puts the person making the "I want" statement in a vulnerable position.

To avoid getting in a vulnerable position, some people avoid being assertive, instead being passive and not stating their wants. They may say, "Whatever you would like to do is fine with me," or "Whatever makes you happy," thereby passing the responsibility for decision making onto the other person. Because of their passivity and consequent lack of vulnerability it is difficult, if not impossible, to form intimate relationships with passive people.

Sometimes people hide behind questions as a way to avoid becoming vulnerable. For example, suppose I were to ask my wife, "Do you want to go to a show tonight?" This sounds like a simple question, but it is more complex than it appears. There may be any one of the following subtexts lurking within it:

"I want to go to the show with you because I'm tired of being in the house."

"I want to go to the show because I want to spend some time with you."

"I want to go to the show because I hear it's a great movie."

So, if I were to just ask the question, "Do you want to go to the show?" my wife might not know what I am really asking. I would be demanding a response from her without having given her all of the information she needs. I am protecting myself from possible disappointment by not stating the real reason behind the question.

When people name something they need, as opposed to something they want, they are making themselves even more vulnerable, because now they are expressing something that isn't negotiable.

A need (in the context of relationship) is something that you must have met in order to continue in the relationship. If my wife states that she needs more time alone with me, and I respond with "I'm too busy, I'll get to you later," you can imagine how that would hurt emotionally. She has taken a great risk, because the issue at stake is not one of temporary disappointment, but of personal rejection.

Control

In order to be sexually vulnerable, a person must not only open up verbally, but must also be willing to relinquish control—both mentally and physically.

Some people like to lose control consciously or mentally by drinking too much alcohol.

Other people like to be in mental control of themselves all of the time; these people typically do not like to become intoxicated. Ideally, we should not be out of control, mentally speaking, but neither should we hold on so tightly that we cannot yield control to someone we trust.

Most people feel extremely vulnerable when they lose physical control of what is happening to them. For example, you probably feel physically vulnerable when you are riding in the passenger seat with a person driving crazily. Sensing your vulnerability, you tighten your whole body, putting your feet to the floorboards as if you were hunting for the brakes. You are physically vulnerable because you don't have control.

Another example of losing control physically is when you are learning to ski. Because you don't know how to stop, you ski very tightly—you may go only a few yards and you are tired; you want to stop and rest. Experienced skiers are loose and fluid; they have the confidence that they can give up control because they know they can get it back by stopping.

The issues of vulnerability and loss of control are particularly relevant to the experience of orgasm. To experience orgasm fully a person must abandon him- or herself mentally and physically for a short period of time. As Helen Singer Kaplan put it in *The New Sex Therapy,* "To function well sexually, the individual must be able to abandon himself to the erotic experience. He must be able to temporarily give up control and some degree of contact with his environment." A person cannot make an orgasm happen on demand, at the snap of his fingers. He must let go involuntarily.

Trust

In order to experience intimacy, you need to be able to trust your partner, to give up control of your actions and feelings, and to go with what gives you pleasure without hesitation. This is what is called being uninhibited sexually. To give up control doesn't mean being out of control and going crazy; it means that you are not holding back and thinking and monitoring what is happening between you and your partner. You are like the skier who is going downhill not holding back and fighting the pull of gravity, but with a sense of abandon, knowing or trusting that he can regain control with a good parallel stop.

Where does the trust come from that enables a person to give up control sexually? It comes from the relationship outside the bedroom. If two people can't trust one another and be emotionally vulnerable, opening up and communicating their feelings verbally, then it will be virtually impossible for them to achieve a quality sexual relationship. If they aren't able to trust each other consciously, they will have a great deal of difficulty giving up control sexually in the most intimate moments, when their overwhelming desire is to fully let go.

Trust requires emotional communication. Obviously, the more a person is vulnerable emotionally, the more he or she can be trusted, because it is difficult to fake emotions. It is much easier to con someone who relies only on logic and verbal persuasion.

To summarize: If people block their emotions in the non-sexual aspects of their relationship, then when they become sexually involved their emotions will stay blocked.

You can't be mere roommates in one part of the house and assume that by changing rooms you will suddenly become lovers.

The greater their degree of emotional vulnerability, the more sexual pleasure a couple will experience.

Emotions or feelings expressed and shared between partners are the lifeblood of a relationship. If you take the emotions out of the sexual experience, it becomes one-dimensional, a body trip that inevitably becomes boring once the novelty wears off.

When someone says that he or she is bored sexually, that tells us that this person is not involved in the sexual experience. One becomes involved sexually by being involved emotionally, and by being vulnerable with the person with whom one is sexually involved.

Commitment

For vulnerability to flourish in a relationship, a sense of trust has to exist. A major requirement for trust is a sense of commitment from both partners. If one person or both are questioning whether or not they want to stay in the relationship, this will greatly affect their ability to let go and become vulnerable, both physically and emotionally. People tend to hold back to protect themselves from being hurt if they sense that their partner has one foot out the door.

In the singles world, the development of trust is difficult. It takes time to get to know someone intimately enough to trust. This is particularly true for adults who have been hurt in previous relationships and who have subsequently developed emotional scar tissue.

The First-Encounter Syndrome

In the fast-paced dating scene, there is little time for trust and openness. Consequently many single people fall prey to a classic sexual conflict which develops as follows. They want their first sexual experience with a partner to be great. This is especially the case if their partner is particularly desirable and attractive. They feel pressure to be highly responsive to their partner, so they are careful not to send a message of dislike or rejection on any level.

The conflict occurs when the couple hasn't spent enough time with each other to establish enough trust so that they can become vulnerable prior to being sexually involved. Without that vulnerability, they may find it difficult to lose control and to be sexually responsive in the way they would like. They try with all their might to let go and experience sexual intimacy, but the experience seems wooden and awkward.

Trust requires an atmosphere of acceptance between partners; this means the absence of judgment. No one is going to open up and be vulnerable if they're afraid of being judged. As I mentioned earlier, without acceptance, very little growth can occur in the relationship.

Lack of Trust Can Create or Intensify Sexual Dysfunctions

Among men who are dating women who are also dating other men, the most common problems include erection difficulties and premature ejaculation. This is particularly true with men who were married for many years and are now newly single. Their brain says that they can or should be able to have sex with a woman regardless of the psychological conditions. "It shouldn't matter if she is sleeping with other men. I should be able to handle that," he tells himself.

Meanwhile he is trying to repress feelings of anxiety and discomfort at being sexually involved when a feeling of trust has not been established in the relationship. And, of course, these feelings manifest themselves in his sexual response. It's as if his penis had begun to talk: "I'm not going to get hard; I don't want to go inside that woman; I don't trust her!" or, "All right, you may be able to get me in there, but you can't make me stay." The same trust problems can affect women, usually in their ability to lose control and respond with an orgasm.

Perceptions

Our attitudes toward our partner's perceptions of the world constitute another important factor in establishing the emotional groundwork for a satisfying sexual relationship. If it is important to accept your lover's emotions as always being valid, the same goes for their perceptions.

Everyone perceives reality differently. When a married couple tells me what has happened or is currently happening in their marriage, each spouse tells a slightly different story. Whose perception is right? When they tell me their stories in one another's presence in a therapy session, they tend to debate their versions of reality:

Wife: It didn't happen that way.

Husband: Yes it did. Now tell the truth, honey.

Wife: I am telling the truth! You are the one who isn't telling the story correctly.

Their conversations can go on like this interminably. Their decibel level increases the longer they talk, because their frustration level is also rising. But their argument isn't producing any agreement as to who is right and who is wrong.

How often, when you have been engaged in this sort of perceptual debate, has your spouse said to you, "You know, honey, I see your point; yes, I'm wrong and you are right."

Rarely.

The answer to the question of whose perception is correct is that they both are correct—or, at least, valid. You may perceive things differently from how everyone else does, but your perception is true for you. In my own marriage, my wife is always right; however she sees things is true for her. It just happens that I don't always agree with her. Here's an example of what I mean:

Let's say that Debra perceives me as taking her for granted, and not appreciating our relationship. Now, assuming that I see things differently, I could react defensively and argue with her, trying to convince her that her perception was wrong. You can imagine what she would do in return. She would defend her position and try to explain how I am wrong.

The more constructive approach, and one that I follow today, is that I validate my wife's perception of me. That is, I don't try to tell her that she is wrong. Instead, I take the position that she is right. It's just that I don't agree. Given that I love her, and that I'm not comfortable knowing that she is displeased, I look for ways to remedy the situation. We try to give each other time and attention to work out a solution. She might say, "Let's plan a trip away someplace where we could give each other some uninterrupted attention."

If I can agree to some of her suggestions, then the problem is handled and we continue being close. This is different from my old style of relating, and produces much better results. A person who constantly tries to convince his lover that her perceptions are wrong is usually someone who is not very secure with his own perceptions. He feels uncomfortable with two different points of view and therefore tries to convert his lover to the one "true" view—his own, of course—so there can be no question about who is right.

Regarding perceptions, it is never a matter of who is right or wrong, but of how to deal with differences in view. It is far better to put your energy into seeking a remedy, rather than trying to decide whose perception is valid. If you don't accept your lover's perceptions, that lover will soon stop communicating anything of importance to you, and cease to be your lover, becoming a room-mate instead.

Listening—A Sexual Aphrodisiac

The next building block to good sex is not a concept, but more of a skill or technique; and it is one of the best sexual aphrodisiacs around. What I'm referring to is good, effective listening.

With clients who are having, or have had an affair, one of the important factors in their attraction to their new lover is often the fact that the lover listened to them; the lover listened in a way that their spouse did not. The lover listened to their problems and the client feels that the lover cares about their emotional experience.

From this ability to listen, a feeling of intimacy develops. A similar intimacy can occur between therapists and their clients; however, in the therapist/client situation there are strict boundaries established. The feeling that someone really cares about you as a person, really understands how you feel, is very powerful, and can be very seductive. This is particularly true if it has been a long time since you experienced a genuinely caring relationship.

If listening plays such a powerful role in the early attraction of lovers, why does listening so often break down in long-term relationships? Most of us were never taught how to listen effectively, especially when someone is communicating emotions that are generally thought of as negative—such as anger, hurt, and fear. In the beginning of a new relationship, those emotions seldom predominate; instead, the emotions we associate with caring and loving move to the fore. After a commitment has been made, people seem to feel that they no longer have to be "on their good behavior." It is safer to let their anger and resentment out, because they aren't as afraid that their partner will leave them.

It is difficult to listen to anger and resentment, especially if we have no experience in doing so; therefore, most of us become defensive. We withdraw behind a newspaper, or we space out in front of the TV, or we have a couple of drinks. Whatever escape route we choose, the result is the same: we stop listening to our lover and intimacy shrinks away. Effective listening can really help a couple maintain a loving relationship.

What is effective listening? In my book *Beyond the Marriage Fantasy*, I go into this in detail. But for the purpose of our present discussion, I will review the major points here.

The three most common mistakes made in listening are the following: (1) Silence with eye contact. This is probably first on the list because as children we were taught to listen this way. We all remember teachers and parents telling us, "Just keep your mouth shut and listen!" The problem with this style of listening is that the speaker is always unsure whether or not his feelings have been heard or understood. This doubt leaves the speaker feeling uncomfortable, if she has communicated information that places her in a vulnerable position. (2) Asking questions of the speaker. This is equally ineffective. The questions may be good, but the timing is always wrong. When you listen to emotional issues, you should just listen. Questions lead the speaker in directions he may not want to go, and they may put the speaker on the defensive. Questions generally get in the way when someone is trying to be emotionally vulnerable. (3) Trying to convince or "sell" the other person on the idea that you are listening and understanding what he says. In this case, the listener uses sounds or phrases to give the idea that he is listening, such as: "Oh, I can really hear where you are coming from" or, "Oh, I've been there" or, "I can really relate to what you are saying." If you've ever been on the receiving end of such comments, you know that you really have no idea whether this feedback is genuine or fake—just a "communication technique" that is automatic and calculated to produce a certain result. For cocktail-party communication, this style of listening may be satisfactory, but not when someone is speaking to you on a personal, emotional level. At its worst, this type of listening response is just plain manipulative, and if we're sensitive at all we can feel downright insulted or resentful.

Active Listening

The style of listening that I recommend in order to let the speaker know that you are really listening has different names: "active listening," "reflective listening," and "effective listening." The name we use doesn't matter much. The essential requirement is simply a verbal acknowledgment of how the speaker feels. By this I don't mean simply saying, "I understand how you feel." The words must match up with a genuine response to what's being communicated. For example, "You really seem upset and hurt about what just happened to you."

Your purpose is to feed back to the speaker what you perceive he or she is feeling emotionally about the subject. Doing this makes the speaker feel understood and cared about. It is not too difficult to understand intellectually how to do this kind of listening; the hard part is to apply the theory. Many people, particularly men, tend to pay attention more to the content of what is being said than to how the speaker feels. Also, many people have a difficult time keeping their own feelings, questions, and opinions to themselves until the speaker has finished; they interrupt the speaker and then try to become the speaker, at which point effective communication ceases. Both people are trying to talk, but no one is listening.

The next time you are with your lover, pay attention to how you listen when he or she talks to you about something meaningful. When she or he is finished talking, does your lover feel closer to you or more distant? Your ability to listen effectively may determine whether this person will continue to be your lover in the future.

Conflict Resolution

The last area that needs to be addressed regarding the building of an emotional groundwork for pleasurable sexual experience is conflict resolution. Simply put, unresolved conflicts inhibit a couple's sexual frequency. It is difficult to be excited about being sexually involved with someone you are angry with because a conflict you had earlier hasn't been resolved.

Couples tend to view conflict as a competition for power. The issue at stake is who will control what happens in the relationship. This kind of conflict creates an adversarial atmosphere in which someone wins and someone loses. The problem is that if one spouse/lover wins and the other feels he or she has lost, then the loser will probably be resentful. This resentment comes back and affects the apparent winner of the conflict later on. In the long run, both of them lose.

One of the most common ways that the "loser" expresses this resentment is by turning off sexually. I've seen many so-called frigid women and men who were in reality only very angry and resentful because they had lost so many conflicts over the years. Don't set up an adversarial relationship with your lover/spouse unless you want to break up or find yourself in divorce court.

Conflicts need to be negotiated to the mutual satisfaction of both partners, with no one leaving the table feeling angry, ripped off, or dominated. Sometimes the negotiation takes ten minutes, sometimes a week. But whatever it takes, the mutual resolve is well worth the effort in the long run. If each partner feels that the other is not out to win, and is concerned that both are satisfied with the accord they reach, then a feeling of respect and comfort with the arrangement is established.

A well-negotiated resolution builds trust, opening doors to new levels of intimacy. Obviously, there will be some conflicts in every relationship that cannot be resolved to the mutual satisfaction of both parties, and in such situations someone needs to give. But, they need to give without holding on to any resentment; otherwise it is not a gift, because it has an emotional price tag connected to it.

Avoiding Confrontation

So far in this discussion of conflict, I've referred to couples who are not afraid to confront issues in their relationships. But what about those who are afraid to be in conflict with someone with whom they're emotionally involved? If both people are passive in the face of conflict, there usually isn't much room for emotional or physical intimacy to grow between them. On the surface, the relationship may appear to be functional, but it is actually boring to the degree that there is emotional censorship. In such cases sex tends to be mechanical, more an expression of glandular function than emotional expression.

When one person is "conflict-phobic" and the other isn't, what follows is a power struggle for intimacy. It usually ends up with the person who wants to deal with issues getting tired of trying to induce the partner to be intimate. That partner withdraws and becomes emotionally apathetic. Whenever one or both partners avoid conflict, the emotional groundwork gets shaky, and sexuality pales.

To summarize: There must be a good emotional atmosphere outside the bedroom in order for there to be a good quality sexual experience in the bedroom in a long-term, committed relationship. The requirements for this kind of healthy emotional atmosphere are: (1) constructive communication of emotions between the partners, without emotional censorship; (2) a high degree of vulnerability in which both partners are able to communicate information that could expose them to being hurt; (3) a strong sense of trust and commitment to the relationship; (4) the ability of each person to listen effectively and acknowledge the other's emotions verbally; and (5) an ability to resolve conflicts so that there is no unfinished emotional business between them when they go to bed at night.

Moving Forward

All of this sounds like a lot to learn. And perhaps it is. But once the process is started, each new skill that we bring to our relationship improves the intimacy we experience. The new levels of trust that we establish are deeply rewarding, providing their own encouragement for learning more about our own and our partner's emotions.

You don't have to walk in the front door one day and start doing all these things. In fact, it could be quite disastrous if you did. Rather, begin by choosing areas to work on that you are most attracted to. This could be because they look easy to you, because you feel a particular need to do something in that area, or because that area intrigues you. You'll be surprised how one new skill leads naturally into another, pulling you along.

When there is a good deal of conflict, it can be a good idea to simply start bringing some of these ideas into your relationship without saying anything about it to your partner. Otherwise, you might be setting yourself up for another argument. Where there is conflict and competition, we have a very strong tendency to reject any new ideas offered by the other person. To accept even a good idea feels like we're giving in or giving up.

So go slowly. If you're in a relationship where there is genuine love, your improved skills will be contagious. At the point that your relationship starts going smoother, share your knowledge openly. Make your efforts mutual and you'll build a relationship that is as secure as it is exciting and sensual.

Whose Job Is It Anyway—
Pleasure and Responsibility

Who is responsible for the quality of a couple's sexual experience? Generally, when I ask this question to groups, the response suggests that both members share equally in the responsibility for what happens. Ideally, that's the right answer. But in our culture, the male is usually taught that he is responsible. He's "not a man" unless he takes responsibility for making sure that his partner experiences an orgasm—preferably several orgasms—by stimulation received through intercourse. Not only is he responsible for her orgasm, but for her whole enjoyment of the sexual experience.

The male's responsibility to "do a good job" puts a great psychological weight on his shoulders. His performance at this "job" determines his image and self-esteem as a man, a lover, or a husband. The health of his male ego depends on how well he can do his job. Make no mistake. This is not a superficial issue. It is a central aspect of the sexual experience for men of the post-women's-liberation age.

Men, Sex, and Responsibility

Many women have told me in the course of counseling that men are selfish sexually; that all they want is one thing—their own pleasure. They don't really care about their partner's pleasure. This may have been true prior to the late 1960s, but I really don't find that it is generally true today.

Many men complain to me that they have tried everything they know of to "make" their wife or lover enjoy sex, but to no avail. The typical complaint runs something like, "Nothing I do seems to work. I've read *The Joy of Sex* and even *More Joy of Sex*, but things between us just don't get any better. I guess I'm inadequate as a lover."

When I tell a man that his partner's sexual problems may not have anything to do with him, he is often surprised and greatly relieved. "You mean I'm not responsible?" he asks. I reply, "No, you could do everything perfectly—right out of the textbook; you could be the perfect lover, and yet things between the two of you might never improve." For a man in this bind, this knowledge lifts a gigantic weight from his shoulders.

Why do men feel so responsible? Part of the answer is that social myth holds that they are supposed to know more about sex than women—and, of course, they themselves want to believe this too. They learned about sex in their health education classes. They may have hung around the locker room and read *Playboy* and *Penthouse.* They've had "expert training"! And since they know so much about sex in general and female sexuality in particular, they must therefore be perfectly qualified to take on the job of being responsible for both their own and their partner's fulfillment.

Let's leave the man for a moment and take a look at how women relate to the issue of sexual responsibility. Most women in our culture relate to sexual responsibility in one of two ways. One way is to feign ignorance of what's below her waist—unaware of what her genitals are all about. She knows little about her own body and her own sexuality. But don't despair. Coming to her rescue, in all his glory, is the male "expert" we have just visited. He will teach her all about sex! Or, so she would like to believe.

This type of woman is perfect for our male sex expert because she is untainted, virgin-like, ready and willing to learn all that he can teach her—and without too much contradiction or conflict. This makes our expert feel safe and secure, because his sexual expertise is never questioned.

The woman who is ignorant about her own sexuality is unable to take responsibility for her needs and wants because she doesn't know what they are in the first place. Unfortunately, she and her partner may become very frustrated and bored sexually, because their situation is that of the blind leading the blind.

There is another kind of woman who is just the opposite of the first—she knows all about her body and her sexuality. Either through masturbation or previous sexual experiences with other men, or both, this woman knows what her sexual needs and wants are. She knows what feels good, and she knows what would make her feel even better.

But while this second type of woman knows a great deal about her own sexuality, she may still be unable to take responsibility for her own sexual pleasure if she is inhibited by fears of being judged as a "bad girl," or worse, a "whore" or "slut." Her fears of judgment may go back to early adolescence.

I remember back in high school that there were some girls— and even groups of girls—that everyone called whores. I never could understand why they were called by this name, because they never really seemed to fit the image. They didn't walk around in fancy or sexy clothes, or drive expensive cars, or charge for their sexual favors. Yet they were put down by their peers. Now, looking back, I realize that these girls may simply have been more sexually developed than the other, more immature girls and boys, such as myself.

Many women are afraid to take responsibility and assert their sexuality for fear that their lover might judge or reject them. Sexual assertiveness by the woman might destroy the man's fantasy of her being virgin-like and untainted. It might bring up questions about her past sexual experience, which could threaten her lover if his own sexual self-esteem is not high.

Another reason why many women who know about their own sexuality won't assert themselves is that they don't want their male lover to feel inadequate at his "job." If the woman says "Not like this, honey, but like this," he could feel criticized and inadequate in his attempt at being the sex expert. He might become defensive and withdraw from being sexually active with her because his ego just can't handle the idea that he has to be told what to do. So, if the woman in this situation likes sex, she assumes that it's best that she not take responsibility. Instead, she keeps her mouth shut and lets him do whatever he thinks is right. From her perspective, some sexual interaction, even if it's not exactly when or how she wants it, is better than no sex at all.

The Perfect Formula for Frustration

Now, let's put this couple in bed together with all their programming about sexual responsibility. The male is like an airplane pilot flying in the fog without any instruments. He touches his partner in one spot and then another, hoping that he is doing the right thing. But, of course, he keeps his feelings of uncertainty to himself. On the surface, everything is under control; he is the expert and he knows what he is doing. Below the surface he is experiencing considerable anxiety and frustration because not only his pride and ego are at stake, but so is the continuation of his relationship with his lover. He is caught in a double bind. On one hand, he wants the sexual experience to be mutually satisfying; on the other, he can't really let himself go and express himself honestly and spontaneously, because he would then be admitting that he really doesn't know what he is doing. He is set up for failure.

His sexual companion is probably saying to herself, "God, I wish he would get it together and do it right!" This is particularly true if this woman is the type who is ignorant of her own body, since she is depending on him to know what he is doing. Now she is finding out that he is not the expert she thought or hoped he was. The woman who knows what she likes sexually is equally frustrated because she feels inhibited in communicating what she wants for the reasons discussed earlier.

The end result for both types of women is that they don't get their needs met, and therefore end up feeling sexually frustrated and unfulfilled. But just like their male counterpart, they keep these feelings hidden and smile as though everything is fine.

For both the man and woman in this scenario, their sexual experience is frustrating and anxiety producing. But given their programming, they are unable to communicate. So they keep making love—with increased frustration and disappointment. Finally, they get to the point where it is less painful simply to avoid sex, so the frequency of their sexual activity decreases. Sometimes this couple might stumble upon a way of interacting sexually that works, but then they tend to stick to the new method until they've worn it out, too. Then they find themselves frustrated and bored to the point where the frequency of their sexual activity decreases even more.

In his book *Male Sexuality*, Bernie Zilbergeld puts it this way: "The man not only conducts the band, but he also plays all the instruments too." The concept that the man is responsible for his own and his partner's sexuality is a barrier to creating a satisfying sexual experience for either of them. The only way that this concept could work is if somehow we could connect the nerve endings in the woman's genitals to the man's brain. Then if he needs to be responsible for her satisfaction, he could be aware of her experience, at least technically. However, there are better ways.

Taking Individual Responsibility

If you examine the idea at all, you'll quickly see how absurd it is for one adult to be responsible for another's subjective experience, be it around sex or any other part of an adult relationship. If I assume responsibility for my wife's experience, sexually or in any other way, then she is no longer an adult. Psychologically I am treating her as a child. This is not emotionally healthy and is frought with emotional booby traps.

A man called Alan came to me for counseling recently. He told me that he always felt responsible for his wife sexually, and that their relationship felt to him like a student-teacher relationship. This was okay for Alan toward the beginning of their relationship, when he wasn't very secure sexually.

After a while, however, Alan began feeling bored and frustrated. He started to resent the idea that his wife had become dependent on him, both to initiate sex, and to bring new creative input into their sexual relationship. He wanted to learn some new and different things so that he could grow sexually. Without her help and partnership, their sexual relationship could not go much further.

This particular couple got out of their sexual rut when they both let go of the old myth that the man had to be the sexually responsible one. Not only was he relieved of what had become a burden to him, but she suddenly felt liberated to discuss her needs and her sexual knowledge with him. The transformation in their relationship was indeed a pleasure for both of them.

What Works?

By now it should be clear that the belief that the man is responsible for what happens sexually is unproductive and destined to lead to trouble. So then, what works? Simply this: the woman is responsible for herself—and her partner is responsible for himself. If you are a man reading this book, you are the foremost authority on your own sexuality and body. You know what feels pleasurable and what doesn't, and that's really as far as your innate knowledge about sex goes. Yes, you may know intellectually about female sexual anatomy and physiology. You may know that stimulating a woman's clitoris may be pleasurable to her. But that is just general information. It is knowing your partners specific needs and desires that will make you an effective, sensitive, caring lover. And only she can provide you with that information.

If you are a woman, you are responsible for your own sexuality. You are the world's best expert when it comes to what pleases you sexually and what doesn't. If you don't know about your own body from a sexual standpoint, then you need to do some research. No man is going to know your body sexually unless you are able to tell him. Don't look around for "Mr. Right," who'll know exactly what to do to turn you on. Such a man doesn't exist. To know your own physiology and your own needs is the fastest and best route to sexual fulfillment.

Some Men Threatened By Responsible Women

Some men I have counseled feel threatened by the idea that they are not responsible for their partner's sexual pleasure. They equate not being responsible with not being needed. I even heard one many tell his partner, "Well, what the hell, why should I be here at all? Go take your vibrator and have a good time."

I try to reassure men by telling them that just because they're not responsible doesn't mean that they're not wanted; it just means that they don't have the map to her territory—she does. Each partner has the map of his or her own territory. Both need to exchange information from their maps freely in order to get where they want to go—being an effective lover. Once you succeed at this, you will be very much needed.

Updating Sexual Communication

Some men relate sexually to women with what I call the "template theory." They develop a pattern of sexual stimulation that worked for satisfying one partner, and then they apply the same pattern to all the other lovers with whom they have sexual encounters. A few women adopt the template theory as well, but it's usually men who do this. A man might say, "Sally, I don't know what the problem is. It worked for Mary Jane. Why don't you like what I'm doing?" This sort of language implies that there is something wrong with Sally because she doesn't respond to his technique. The problem here is obvious. The man is failing to see that Sally is not Mary Jane. She is a sexually unique individual.

The man in this example is failing to recognize that everyone—every man and woman—is sexually unique. What is pleasurable for one person may not be pleasurable for another. Moreover, every person changes from one day to the next. What felt good sexually one night for my wife may be too sensitive, too aggressive, or too something else the next.

Our hormones change. Our moods change. Our likes and dislikes change. We're fortunate that this is so; otherwise our sex lives would become predictable and boring. So the reality is that I don't really know what my wife may like at any given time when I approach her sexually. I know some basic things, but for the specifics, I need some communication from her, either verbal or nonverbal. I need an open mind so I can be sensitive to the nuances of the moment.

In the end, taking responsibility for your own sexuality boils down to the use of two very simple but powerful messages: "I want," or "I don't want"—or some variation on these themes. As I discussed in my previous book, *Beyond the Marriage Fantasy*, there is nothing quite so effective as the use of "I" messages during intimate communications outside the sexual context.

While it is easy to say that we should clearly tell our lovers what we want and don't want, in practice this is often difficult to do. I am not suggesting that you be more sexually demanding of your partner. But you do need to express your desires clearly. Then, if your partner *chooses* to respond—and it is his or her *choice*—that partner will be better equipped to please you!

In some long-term relationships (and this obviously applies to some marriages), the individuals at one time communicated what they specifically enjoyed, but never updated the information as it changed. What felt good the first time may have stopped feeling pleasurable after the second or third or five hundredth time, but that information wasn't expressed. Talking to your partner isn't a one-time proposition; it's an ongoing process.

Ideas that Limit Communication

There are may factors which teach us that its not okay to communicate about sex. In our society, families rarely talk about sex together. Yet, we also know that in families where sex is discussed more openly, young people are more likely to feel that it's okay to share their sexual feelings openly with their marriage partners.

One of the harmful communication myths that our society supports is that saying clearly what you want is selfish, and selfishness is bad. Saying what you want can indeed be selfish—if you also demand that the other person only satisfy your needs. Such an attitude makes the other person a slave to your needs and has no place in an intimate relationship, or any relationship.

Communication and Trust

Can you trust your lover or spouse to take responsibility for his or her sexuality? If you can, then you don't have to worry about guessing what he or she wants and needs. You have the basis for a high level of sexual pleasure in a long-term, intimate relationship.

If you can't trust your partner to take responsibility for him- or herself, then you will tend to become preoccupied with thinking about your partner's sexual experience. This kind of thinking is anything but an aphrodisiac. It usually runs along these lines: "I hope she likes what I'm doing to her," or, "I'm afraid that I'm taking too long and that he's getting bored," or, "I think she is just making love to me because she feels guilty." Such thoughts simply get in the way of feeling the pleasure of the moment.

One man told me that when his wife was performing oral sex on him he believed that she was doing so only for his pleasure, and that she did not enjoy it. So whenever he found himself in that situation, he would start thinking about her not enjoying herself and start feeling guilty. This quickly robbed him of the pleasure he might have experienced.

In a therapy session one day, he asked his wife, "Do you enjoy giving me pleasure that way?" And she replied "Sure, it turns me on to feel you getting so excited by something I'm doing. Plus I love you and I like to give you pleasure." Once he heard that, he stopped worrying about his partner and just enjoyed the experience to the fullest, confident that they were sharing a mutual pleasure.

Eroticism and Trust

When you can trust that your partner is taking responsibility for his or her sexuality and is comfortable doing what gives pleasure; when you can trust that your partner will tell you if he or she is uncomfortable or wants to do something different, then you're free from worrying and can enjoy whatever you are doing or whatever he or she is doing to you.

Taking responsibility for your own sexuality opens up new vistas of pleasure and freedom for your partner, since then he or she can stop worrying about you and stop feeling responsible for your pleasure. In sexuality as elsewhere, trust is built on good, open, loving communication of our needs. Sometimes it takes time to build that trust. Sometimes it happens very quickly. In any case it is a tremendous liberation and one of the single most important steps to take toward a satisfying sexual relationship.

When Sex Becomes a
Goal-Oriented Activity

We are all familiar with goals—academic goals, professional goals, financial goals, and personal goals. In these areas of our lives goals and goal-setting can certainly be helpful. But where sex is concerned, goals can create more problems than they solve. I've known couples who had small sexual goals that only mildly inhibited their sexual pleasure. And I've known couples who had large sexual goals that turned them into sexual cripples. In my experience, when it comes to sex, more and bigger goals means more and bigger problems.

Goals always relate to the future. If we are mentally in the future, then that means we're not in the present. In order to experience sexual pleasure we must be focused in the present moment.

When our attention drifts into the future, we become distracted. Who knows what is going to happen down the road? The phone may ring or the children may wake up and come in. Some people are so busy worrying about the future that they never get there. They miss all the pleasure of the moment. The future only exists in imagination. Seize the moment!

Consider the following story. A couple is on vacation, driving from Los Angeles to New York City. As they travel, all they think about is the "Big Apple"; they pay little attention to the sights along the way. What might have been an enjoyable drive turns into a grind—day after day of meaningless drudgery. By the time they reach New York, they are so accustomed to being out of the present—anticipating and complaining—that they are unable to relax and enjoy themselves. Moreover, they spend all their time comparing their actual experiences of the city to their expectations of it. They allow little space for spontaneity, so their experience of the city is deadened.

The time comes to leave and they start reviewing how well their experience matched their expectations. And of course they decide that they saw very little that measured up. Physically they were in New York but mentally and emotionally they were never present. In the end their trip was equivalent to a marathon sleep-walk.

In a gift shop, I once saw a poster that said, "Life is a journey, not a destination." Like life, sex is a journey.

The Destructive Definition of Foreplay

One word in our sexual vocabulary epitomizes this goal-oriented thinking—"foreplay." Foreplay, of course, is sexual activity such as kissing, hugging, fondling, holding, touching and caressing; it also includes verbal expressions of endearment like, "I love you. You look really beautiful and sexy tonight." The words can refer to all kinds of tactile and verbal sensual stimulation of your lover.

When I ask clients or students the purpose of foreplay, they usually define it as a necessary activity that precedes having sex. What they are really saying is that foreplay is the preliminary to intercourse. The word itself implies this: "Foreplay" by definition is play that goes before something else.

Among teenagers who have not yet had their first experience of intercourse, foreplay is the sum total of the sexual activity that takes place. When I was a teenager this was called "making out" or "necking," or "petting." Whatever it was called, it was great!

We generally understood that intercourse wasn't yet acceptable, even though the males might try for it.

The understanding that intercourse probably wasn't going to happen forced couples to pay attention to the present. But was there ever a lot of pleasure in the moment! Most people who "made out" in this way enjoyed themselves even though they might have been somewhat frustrated if they didn't experience an orgasm.

Something changes in a relationship once the green light to have intercourse goes on. Once the couple is committed to each other or married, and intercourse is possible, then all the foreplay they once enjoyed seems like some adolescent activity that is merely in the way of real adult sex—namely, intercourse.

I sometimes think that the amount of time a couple spends in foreplay shrinks in direct proportion to the length of time they have been together. When the amount of foreplay decreases the amount of time spent kissing, fondling, touching, and holding each other decreases. Foreplay becomes subordinate to the "big event"—intercourse. Couples in this state might ask these sorts of questions: "Are you turned on yet?"; "Are you ready?"; "Come on, let's get it on"; "I have to go to work tomorrow"; "Good, let's stop this fooling around and have sex."

If the time a couple spends engaged in foreplay decreases, then their experience of pleasure, touching quality, eroticism, and sensuality will also decrease. When people complain about marital sex being "without spice," the first remedy they should consider is increasing the quantity and quality of their touching and foreplay—even to the point of agreeing that it won't necessarily end in intercourse.

Is foreplay sex? Of course it is sex! If, during foreplay, you're thinking about the next step—intercourse—you have effectively removed yourself from the pleasure of the moment. While intercourse is an important part of sex, it is no more the whole of sex than the seeds are the whole of the apple.

Our culture has decided that only intercourse itself is "real sex." This idea may stem from ancient religious programming which decreed that the only valid purpose for sex was reproduction. If sex is indeed for making babies, then intercourse is clearly the focus of sex. But if sex is for pleasure, then this concept is obsolete. Defining "foreplay" as something apart from, preliminary to, and less than full sex may be one of the single most destructive ideas our society has about relationships.

The Fatal Equation

Let's go back to our vacationers dreaming of New York. When, in the course of their lovemaking, a couple finally reaches intercourse, is their focus on what's happening during intercourse? Probably not. They're on to the next goal—orgasm. They're thinking about "The Big O." They may be saying to themselves, or to each other, "Did you come?"; "Uh, oh, I'd better slow down or I'm going to come," "I'm coming too fast," or "I'd better hurry up and come." This sort of dialogue focuses on the future, not the present, and reveals how the sexual pleasure of the moment is being missed.

Once the couple has achieved the short-term goals of foreplay, intercourse, and orgasm, they then feel they have arrived at their final destination. They've achieved their goal. We have an equation that looks like this: F(oreplay) + I(ntercourse) = O(rgasm). In surveys of couples I see, I have found this to be the most common pattern for sexual activity. It is this pattern that I call "meat-and-potatoes sex."

Kicking the Habit of Rigidity

After a couple experience goal-oriented sex for a period of time, they might begin to wonder if they aren't missing something. It's like eating junk food for the quick relief of one's hunger—it satisfies the appetite, but doesn't provide much in the way of real nourishment. To draw a parallel, if a couple's sex life is made up of "junk sex," they may suffer from a different kind of malnourishment, called "pleasure deprivation." While there is nothing wrong with a "quickie" now and then, when goal-oriented sex becomes a habit, it's time to take a new look at what you're doing.

When a couple think of sex in a goal-oriented way, they too often assume that foreplay must end in intercourse, and intercourse isn't complete unless there is orgasm. Imagine getting on a train in San Francisco and going all the way to New York without any stop-overs or side trips. That would be fine if it happens to be a business trip. But if the whole purpose of the trip is pleasure, wouldn't it make more sense to let the journey unfold at its own pace and in its own way? Maybe the highlight of the entire trip is a canyon in Utah or a waterfall in Colorado. Maybe we don't need to "go all the way" to New York at all!

In *Male Sexuality*, Bernie Zilbergeld says that one of the common male sexual myths is that good sex is a linear progression of increasing excitement terminating in orgasm. Sex, according to this view, should be a process of continually increasing excitement and passion. Sexual arousal should continue to build. Not only must we go all the way, but we must do so with a certain speed and intensity, somewhat like a steam train leaving the station.

But when we pursue sex with this kind of goal orientation our sexual relationship becomes rigid; and when rigidity sets in, the relationship becomes predictable and boring. Instead of following the same predictable pattern, we need to break up the pattern and develop more flexible ways of interacting sexually. When I suggest to couples that they learn to be more flexible in their sex life, they immediately picture weird and kinky activities. I'm not adverse to such activities if the couple can be comfortable with them, but you don't have to go to extremes just to break the monotony!

I often advise people who are caught in the "meat-and-potatoes" routine to vary the sexual options they currently enjoy. I suggest that they treat sex as a leisurely activity, with breaks for resting, laughing, and talking. And I introduce the possibility that orgasm doesn't have to be the main goal. Many couples learn that their greatest sexual pleasure comes when they concentrate most of their attention on kissing, fondling, and touching each other. Maybe this activity flows into intercourse, then goes back to kissing and touching again. They might also touch and kiss each other to the point of mutual satisfaction, having orgasms manually or orally, never engaging in intercourse.

Breaking ourselves of the habit of goal-oriented sex opens doors to whole vistas of possibility. We never need do the same thing twice.

Sex Doesn't End with Orgasm

Another example of rigidity in a relationship—and one that puts a great deal of emotional pressure on men—is when the man ejaculates before his partner has experienced an orgasm. Often, once the male ejaculates, the whole sexual experience comes to a crashing halt. The man says, "I'm tired now, I'm going to sleep," or, "I'm sorry, maybe next time." Why is this? If it is 1:00 PM, why is he going to sleep?

The answer is partly physiological. Following orgasm, men often do naturally feel sleepy. But because of this tendency, women sometimes think of men as sexually selfish because they don't seem to care about their partner's satisfaction. Whether he is in fact being selfish or not (and this is, no doubt, sometimes the case), the man may also retire from sex play out of a feeling of inadequacy.

Many men, and women too, have a rigid idea of how they are supposed to experience orgasm. The man may think that once he ejaculates and loses his erection, he will be unable to pleasure and satisfy his partner, because he believes that the only right or normal way to stimulate a woman to orgasm is with his penis. Once he has ejaculated, if he is unable to have another erection right away, he feels inadequate and may go to sleep partly out of embarrassment.

Rigid thinking of this kind limits our sexual experiences and puts unnecessary pressure on us, which of course only further limits the amount of sexual pleasure we can experience.

A more flexible attitude, and one that allows for more pleasure, might be the following: Whatever way a woman can experience orgasm is right and normal. So, if a man loses his erection after ejaculation, what's wrong with using his hands or mouth to stimulate his partner? Either of these methods might be as pleasurable for her as intercourse. Once again, this need not evolve into another rigid pattern, but it certainly gives the man more options and the relationship more variety.

A woman in this situation can ask her partner to give her more stimulation so that she won't feel frustrated and possibly resentful. She may even do so by initiating further petting or performing oral sex on him. If this is done in a loving and sensitive way, making sure the man understands that she still feels him to be sexy and a source of erotic stimulation, she may avoid the problems that flow from the man feeling inadequate.

Goals Create Anxiety

In addition to distracting us from the present, sexual goals create another major problem—emotional anxiety. The degree of anxiety that arises during sex depends on the importance the individual places on achieving a goal—the more it's wanted, the more anxiety exists.

When you really want to do well, or you know your score on a test will make the difference between a final grade of A or B, how do you feel emotionally? You probably feel nervous, pressured, and anxious. These same emotions inhibit sexual pleasure.

Usually, when a couple "work" at trying to improve their sexual relationship, the harder they try, the worse the problem becomes. Finally, they may simply give up working at their sex life out of pure frustration and disappointment. The problem of goal orientation and its associated anxiety is particularly common with men who are successful, who are high achievers. This type of male is accustomed to working hard for what he wants in life. He succeeds by having goals and sticking to them with determination and perseverance.

When he applies the same attitudes that made him a success at the office to his sex life, they backfire. The goal-oriented person can be so caught up in attaining future rewards—and in delaying his immediate gratification in favor of a bigger prize—that he or she forgets that sex is about pleasure and enjoyment in the here and now.

Sex and Bonding

When a couple's sex life is ruled by goals, another problem is created in terms of their ability to intimately bond with one another. There are three ways in which a couple can intimately connect or bond: intimate verbal communication, touching, and intercourse.

Intimate Verbal Communication. Since most people have had little experience and no training in "boudoir talk," couples have difficulty bonding in this way. Also, when time is limited—as it so often is for couples with children, or in the case of partners with busy work schedules—this form of bonding seldom occurs.

Touching. A couple can bond intimately through physical expressions of affection. Without anyone saying a single word, a pat, holding hands, or a caress can say much about how lovers feel about each other. In the beginning of a new relationship, there is usually a lot of holding, touching, and kissing. In fact, some couples just can't stop touching each other, which makes others who aren't experiencing much affection in their lives very uncomfortable.

At the same time that this new couple is being affectionate with each other, they are also being sexual with one another. Often this general outside-the-bedroom affection leads to sexual activity inside the bedroom.

In the beginning of a new relationship, this sequence of touching through petting to intercourse may set a continuing precedent. The couple is unwittingly establishing a goal. An assumption is being ingrained that once general expression of affection begins, it somehow must end with intercourse. This pattern is so widespread and deep that many women are afraid of being judged as a tease or as leading men on if they are affectionate but not interested in getting sexually involved.

When a couple loses interest in sex, they usually also stop being as physically affectionate as they once were. As the realities of life start to interfere with a new relationship, as the novelty wears off, then sex doesn't occur as spontaneously or as frequently. In a vicious circle, as sexual frequency diminishes, so does the amount of physical affection expressed by the couple. Typically, the longer a couple has been together, the less affection is exchanged between them. This is due to many factors, but one of them may well be the goal-oriented attitude that touching must lead to intercourse.

Intercourse. The third way a couple bonds is, of course, through sexual relations—primarily intercourse. Since the couple hasn't the time or ability to bond verbally, and since they are beginning to restrict their expressions of affection (because they believe that affection must lead to sexual activity and they don't have time for that), sexual intercourse itself becomes the primary vehicle by which they express their love for one another.

Expressing love through sexual activity is certainly neither wrong nor a problem, but if it becomes the only means of expression, then too much psychological weight is placed on the sex act, thereby turning something that is supposed to be fun, relaxing, and enjoyable into a proving ground for the couple's love for each other. This psychological pressure often causes the sexual relationship itself to deteriorate.

Something similar may happen when the couple try to have a baby and they are working really hard at getting pregnant. They make sure it is the right time of the month, the right hour of the day, and they check her temperature to see if she is ovulating. When all those variables are in correct alignment, then it's time to have intercourse—whether you really feel like it or not. Again, something that is supposed to be fun and relaxing becomes work—a goal-oriented experience.

If you are one of the many people who has done this, it may take you a while to enjoy sex again after the goal of reproduction has been achieved.

What happens if the partners don't talk to each other intimately, are not very affectionate, and now are not very sexual with each other?

They become roommates. They may or may not get along with each other, and their relationship withers emotionally. How long a relationship can exist without love bonding depends on the couple. One thing is certain: if bonding is absent, eventually a point is reached where the relationship is emotionally dead, and there is no way to revive the old feelings. Daily maintenance of a love relationship is necessary to keep it vibrant and alive. The more variety and balance there is in the intimate bonding—given the realities of daily life, like children, work, social activities, and so on—the easier it will be for the couple to maintain a high degree of intimacy.

Goal-oriented sexuality can greatly interfere with the frequency of sex. Often a lover will say, "I'm too tired tonight, honey," but then stay up and read a book or watch TV instead. This sort of response and action makes sense to the person who views a sexual relationship as a series of goals to be achieved. After working all day trying to produce, perform, and achieve, the last thing such a person would want to do would be to continue working when he or she was finally at home and going to bed.

Sex, Relaxation, and Pleasure

Some of the better times for me sexually have been when I'm physically tired, such as after skiing all day, or playing tennis, or jogging. I'm physically tired but very relaxed, and mentally alert. Being relaxed is the key to sexual pleasure. We are at our best when there is no pressure to put on a sexual production or performance, when we are simply being open to receiving and giving sexual pleasure. I see sexual pleasure as a way of re-energizing myself. Instead of being an energy-draining experience, it's a way to recharge my batteries.

Incredible though it may seem, many people have difficulty accepting the idea that we should allow ourselves to have pleasure. I ask couples, "How much pleasure do you have in your life?" I don't mean the kind of pleasure that you experience by working at something like gardening or running five miles—this is (to varying degrees) a goal-oriented activity. I mean the kind of pleasure in which you are able to just kick back and enjoy an experience without having to produce or achieve anything—the kind of pleasure you get from just sitting on a beach or relaxing in a hot tub.

For many people, particularly men, this kind of pleasure actually evokes feelings of guilt. Tapes are always playing in the back of their minds telling them they "should" be producing, achieving, and making something happen. It's just not okay—their tapes keep telling them—to experience pleasure unless you have done something to achieve it.

Sex gives us the opportunity to soak up pleasure without having to achieve anything. I often hear women with infants or small children complain about how tired they are from giving all day. I hear similar complaints from women who put out a great deal of energy at work all day and then continue to give of themselves to their children and husbands, working at the jobs of being wife and mother.

When such a woman goes to bed at night and her husband initiates sexual activity, she may decline due to fatigue. She sees sexual activity as a continuation of her day—more work and giving of her energy. By that time she has none left. She can't say no to her work or her children, but she can say no to her husband—and hopefully, he will understand.

By saying no to her husband, she is also saying no to herself. She is cutting off one of the few, and probably the best, opportunities to take care of herself emotionally and physically. She is abandoning one of her primary opportunities to experience pleasure.

Taking advantage of the opportunity would require a change in her way of viewing sexual activity with her husband. Instead of seeing sex with her husband as a time when she has to give some more, she could look at it as a time when he could give her sexual pleasure in whatever form she prefers. Once her batteries have been charged a little, she probably will want to give pleasure back to him, if there is no pressure for her to do so. Perhaps, on another occasion, it would be the husband's turn to receive. When we view sex as a nurturing experience rather than as a drain, it becomes a great way to prevent emotional burnout, both for the individuals concerned and for their relationship.

It is extremely beneficial for a couple to have a flexible attitude regarding the ways in which they make love to each other. Suppose that Jane is physically tired from the day's activities, but John has more energy; he does the initiating and more of the giving sexually, while Jane allows herself mostly to receive pleasure. On another occasion, the situation could be just the reverse. Sometimes they may both have a lot of energy and will both be very involved in giving and receiving; sometimes both are tired and just hold and touch each other because neither has much energy to give.

Again, the key to a vibrant sex life is flexibility. Sexual goals create a sense of rigidity, which limits your sexual expression and behavior. Rigidity cripples you sexually, preventing you from varying your sexual behavior to adapt to the varying conditions that occur over the course of a long-term relationship.

Flexibility in the way a couple interact sexually also allows for the development of something called "synergy." Synergy is a word coined by Carl Jung to describe the situation in which two systems working together produce results greater than the sum of their actions when working separately. Synergy occurs frequently in a relationship that is healthy and vibrant—and the word is especially apt in describing a fulfilling and pleasurable sexual exchange. Because synergy is by definition more than the logical combination of the parts, it is not something that you can decree or prescribe. It comes upon you unexpectedly, and is thus synonymous with flexibility and openness.

Awareness Experience: Moving from Goals to the Pleasure of the Moment

It is easy to see how goal orientation stands in the way of sexual pleasure in the moment. But we are a very goal-oriented society and this way of thinking has been deeply ingrained in us. How can we free ourselves of it? One way is by getting in touch with the primal sensations of our bodies.

In recent years, psychotherapists have learned that there are simple mental techniques that can be used to renew our focus on bodily sensations that might otherwise be blocked by our thoughts. The following is an exercise I've found to be most helpful for the couples and individuals with whom I work in my clinical practice.

To prepare yourself, get into a comfortable position, either sitting in a chair with both feet on the floor and hands resting gently on your knees; or lying on your back, hands at your sides and legs uncrossed. If you can do so, have a friend read the following instructions all the way through so you can become completely familiar with them before you start. You may then wish to keep this book beside you, with this exercise marked so that you can easily refer to it as you go along.

Take your time. Do each part of this exercise in a slow and leisurely way. Close your eyes and let them stay closed until you finish this exercise.

Turn your attention to the way your body feels. Say out loud the different things you feel inside your body. Be as specific as you can. For example, you might say, "I feel tension in my neck," or "I feel the weight of my wristwatch on my arm." Say whatever you feel, describing whatever sensations you experience, no matter how insignificant they may seem to you.

As you become aware of the different feelings in your body, let yourself be aware of your environment. Describe your awareness. For example, you might say, "I'm aware of the neighbor mowing his lawn," or "I'm aware of the children playing in the next room." Take your time and explore your awareness of the environment, verbally describing your awareness.

Now, express aloud all the thoughts that you are thinking. Say out loud everything that crosses your mind, such as, "I'm thinking about eating dinner," or even "I'm thinking about thinking." Take your time. Explore and verbalize your thoughts in a leisurely way. Notice if you become conscious of any thoughts that you censor or repress back into your unconscious.

Turn your attention once more to what you feel in your body. Notice any changes from the first time you focused on your body. Have parts that were tense before relaxed? See if you can become aware of even the smallest of sensations, such as the pressure of your glasses on your nose, the slight tingling of your necklace around your neck, or the rhythmic expansion and contraction of your breathing.

Now open your eyes.

Generally, when people have finished this awareness experience, they feel much more relaxed than when they started, because they have acknowledged the messages that their bodies are sending them.

The point of this exercise is to allow you to explore the three things on which you can focus your attention during sexual activity—

(1) Your body's feelings or sensations,

(2) Your awareness of the environment, and

(3) Your thoughts.

Sensation, awareness, and thinking constitute three levels of consciousness. We go in and out of these different levels of consciousness constantly, and the amount of time we spend in one or another can vary tremendously. Contrary to the common assumption, we have a choice about which conscious mode we are in at any given moment.

Choosing Your Focus of Consciousness

During sexual activity, if you are touching or being touched, and you are in the thinking mode, it will be difficult for you to really feel the touch. And, if while touching or being touched, you are aware of what your partner is doing, as if you were a spectator, or if you focus your attention on sounds coming from another room, it will likewise be difficult for you to enjoy the touching you are giving or receiving from your partner. If you are in the body sensations mode, then you will feel the stimulation to its fullest.

The most pleasurable mode of consciousness for sex is the feeling or body sensations mode. You want to be aware of all the sensations you feel—warmth, coolness, the smooth or rough parts of the body, the texture of hair, and so on. Too often couples overlook these sensations and only seek orgasm—"the big turn-on"; they are so caught up in achieving the goal that they miss all the pleasure along the way. What we are talking about here is sensuality, an ingredient that is missing in the sexual relationships of all too many couples.

During sex, you may be focusing on your body feelings, but thoughts or an awareness of the environment may distract you. If this occurs, simply acknowledge the thought or the awareness. As strange as this may sound, that is the best way to free yourself of it. Let yourself become aware of it, then let it go. Go back to what you are feeling sexually—the choice is your mind's, not your body's.

After they've been together a few years, some couples tend to forget how they once were able to be sexual involved in many unlikely places, with many distractions in the environment—when they were "parking" by the side of the road; in the college dorm room; in her parents' living room when the rest of the family was (hopefully) asleep, and so on. It didn't seem to matter then that the conditions weren't ideal. Why? Because the desire to share physical intimacy with the other person was far stronger than any inhibiting distraction from the environment.

Interest overcomes obstacles. When we're listening to a speaker who is boring and speaks in a monotone we may fidget and daydream; the least disturbance seizes our attention. But a dynamic speaker keeps us on the edge of our seat, and at the end of the talk we don't know where the time went. The same principle applies to a sexual relationship. When someone has to have all the conditions absolutely perfect in order to be engaged sexually, it can be fruitful to ask if that person truly wants to be sexually involved in the first place.

Some people find that small amounts of alcohol or marijuana help them focus on the feelings they are experiencing during sex. They describe themselves as being "loose" after indulging—more able to be involved in the pleasure of the moment.

Drugs shut off the "critical parent" in your thinking—the part of you that is full of "don'ts" and "shoulds." It allows the natural child in you to be more spontaneous and uninhibited, to just let go and flow with what feels pleasurable without passing judgment on whether it's right or wrong, good or bad. Drugs can act as a short-cut in developing this type of sexual freedom.

I definitely don't advocate the use of drugs or alcohol for better sex. The reason is simple: the same state of mind can be achieved through awareness of the factors outlined in the experience above.

Our bodies are wonderful teachers, and our brains naturally contain all the chemical ingredients necessary to a blissful experience. As you free yourself from the sexual problems that your upbringing or society may have implanted, you are free to experience the full extent of sexual pleasure without any artificial stimulation. With this knowledge, you possess a biological pharmacology of pleasure that no amount of artificial chemical stimulation through drugs or alcohol can give you, and it's all built right into your system!

Who Goes First?—
Initiating Sex

Many people—single and married alike—find it difficult to initiate sex. Sexual initiation is often the key to a couple's entire sexual relationship, since it is the moment at which the decision is made to create a sexual relationship. When the frequency of sex diminishes, initiation is one of the first things we examine. But initiation may be an issue even if sex is not infrequent.

In our culture, we have many "dos" and "don'ts" about initiation, rules that structure and limit it. Who wrote these rules? No matter what the answer to that question, we should all recognize that we needn't blindly adhere to them. If the rules get in our way, we are free to rewrite them.

In chapter one we looked at the history through which our early concepts about sex are implanted. We saw how difficult it can be to replace those concepts with ones that really work for us. One of the first concepts that young boys and girls learn about sex is that men should be aggressive and women should be passive. I first learned this in a fifth grade dance class where it was made quite clear that I was expected to ask the girl to dance, not the other way around.

I can still remember the anxiety I felt. Little did I know that this was the beginning of my education in sexual relations with the opposite sex. And I can only imagine how uncomfortable it was for many of the girls to sit and wait, hoping that someone would ask them to dance. When not asked, they must have felt inadequate and publicly humiliated. I couldn't see the picture from their perspective. All the girls looked cool as cucumbers to me. I was the one who was insecure and nervous—or so I thought.

And so a precedent is set. Here were planted the seeds of some very basic beliefs, that the man, if he really is a man, is always trying to "get" the girl; meanwhile, she is always saying no to his advances trying to be passive, disinterested, cool. This is the classic sexual "dance" that men and women have played out for a long time. Men are programmed to initiate. They are supposed to come on to the girl and make things happen, ask her out for a date, then push for having sex with her. It is all expected of him. She can't seem too interested or desirous, otherwise she won't be seen as a "nice girl."

If a reversal of this pattern takes place, and the woman is sexually aggressive while the man is passive, other people tend to judge them in various ways. All sorts of threats and fears come into play, like, "You don't want to threaten the man again and have him lose his erection now, do you?"; "You don't want to be seen as a whore and a slut"; "You don't want him to think you push this hard with all the men you meet, do you?"

Society Discourages Assertive Women

It's just not generally acceptable for a woman to be sexually aggressive in our society. While individual women have succeeded in liberating themselves from this sexist stereotyping, it is very much alive in the culture as a whole.

I am reminded again of the girls in my junior high school who were labeled whores. As I said earlier, these girls were probably just more sexually mature than the boys who were characterizing them. They weren't going along with the stereotype of being nice, passive girls sexually, so they took a lot of heat for just being different. But even though many of the boys put them down at school, we would go over to their houses after school, confirming the old double standard again. Looking back, it seems likely that having their sexuality stigmatized at that time inhibited them sexually as adults.

The issues surrounding women's sexual assertiveness come into focus in what is commonly called the madonna/whore dichotomy. The paradox here is that the man may crave a woman who is virgin-like: innocent, aloof from sex, concerned only about motherhood and domestic issues. At the same time, he also wants a woman who is passionate, expressive. Obviously, there is a conflict. If the woman tries to meet one set of expectations, she finds herself clashing with the other set. When she tries to be sexually aggressive and expresses her sexual desires, she is criticized for not being more madonna-like; if she represses her sexuality, then she is accused of being frigid.

Many women avoid this double bind by simply shutting down their sexuality all together. They may dress and act in a way that minimizes their sexuality. They may fulfill their need for touching and loving through their children or by eating. The husband may then go outside the marriage to get his sexual needs met by way of a "whore-like" woman, i.e., a woman who "enjoys" sex. He then has his "madonna" at home and his "whore" outside.

This is the sort of arrangement that is encouraged by the Victorian sexual standards we discussed earlier. In Victorian times such an arrangement was tacitly accepted. Today it still occurs, but it is by no means accepted because it creates a great deal of pain and turmoil when the wife discovers what is going on. The acknowledgment of the affair is often the catalyst for divorce (though not its true cause).

This madonna/whore syndrome surfaces in many relationships when the woman becomes pregnant, or soon after the first child is born. Once she is a mother, the woman is no longer a sexual person in some men's view—and in the view of some women, too. This may be one of the contributing factors in the decline of sexual frequency during pregnancy or once a child is born. It might also account for the many men who have affairs at this point in the marriage. They can't see their wives as sexual now that the wives are "madonnas."

Men and Sexual Assertiveness

If the woman is sexually aggressive, the man may become sexually passive. What effect does this role reversal have on him? The whole idea of a male being passive, in whatever context, is culturally unacceptable. It goes against our stereotypical concept of "manliness."

When a man becomes passive, his self-esteem and self-image may become deflated. But most important, it puts him in a vulnerable position. He is not in control, sexually speaking. For many men—particularly for those who are not confident about their own sexuality—it is very frightening not to be in control of what is happening sexually. So a cycle is started. When the man becomes sexually passive, his sexual self-esteem goes downhill. The lower his self-esteem, the harder and more risky it is for him to become the initiator of sex. So he remains sexually passive—and the cycle perpetuates.

There is also a physiological component within this process. Studies of male humans and lower primates under various conditions suggest a relationship between male testosterone secretion and certain psychological states. Low self-esteem, depression, humiliation, and rejection are associated with a dramatically lowered testosterone level. With a lower testosterone level, the male's ability to be aggressive is inhibited; also, his sexual desire is reduced.

If you are a man caught in this cycle, it is vital that you break out. You do this by developing higher self-esteem outside of a sexual relationship in which you have to be the aggressor. If you don't do this, you are setting yourself up for failure. The classic example of this cycle occurs when a newly divorced or separated man tries to establish a new relationship with a woman. His confidence is very shaky. He has left the shelter of a long-term marriage or relationship and now finds himself out in the cold, frightening, single world. He might also be suffering from a sense of failure due to the breakup of his marriage or relationship. Clearly, his confidence is at a low ebb.

Where does he go to meet a woman? Probably the local "swinging singles" bar. This has to be one of the most intimidating places for a man who doesn't have much confidence. To operate in the bar scene requires an excellent sense of self and an ability to aggressively persuade women. Even with those attributes, the experience can be disappointing. Most likely, our man leaves the scene feeling worse than when he walked in.

Behavior styles that are rigidly aggressive or rigidly passive can deaden sexual pleasure. Synergy becomes impossible. When I hear one member of a couple insist that he or she wants the partner to be more aggressive, I usually find that this is not what is really wanted at all. Being aggressive implies not caring about the other person's feelings. All the aggressive person cares about is getting what he or she wants. Being aggressive in bed is like saying, "Come here, woman, and make love to me. I don't care if you really want to—that doesn't matter."

What does produce intimacy, in the relationship as a whole, and in sex in particular, is assertiveness. Assertiveness is saying what you want, but without the expectation that you will always get what you want.

It is easier for men to make the transition to assertiveness, because assertiveness doesn't altogether clash with our culture's concept of masculinity. However, for men who have been accustomed to getting their own way, the switch to the assertive stance can be difficult and threatening because it brings with it the possibility of losing control.

For those men who have been sexually passive, the switch to assertive behavior is perhaps more difficult. They have been accustomed to playing it safe with women, taking few risks. Sometimes, though, in trying to be more assertive, a passive man becomes aggressive because of built-up resentments acquired in his experience of being passive for so long.

The Effects of Women's Choices

For women who have been traditionally and stereotypically passive in sexual relationships, the transition to assertiveness is very difficult. Years of unresolved and unconscious resentment may have accumulated. This may surface as a woman becomes assertive, leading to critical and dominating behavior, for which she will be judged. If she stumbles in her first inexpert attempts at self-assertion, she may feel guilty and return to the safety of passivity. Even women who are naturally and confidently sexually assertive run the risk of being judged "cheap."

Often, when I suggest to a woman that she make the first move by asking a man out to lunch, or to meet him for a drink after work, she is afraid that he might feel threatened by her role reversal. This is a concern also in the context of the bedroom. A man may talk and fantasize about wanting his partner to be sexually assertive and initiate the lovemaking, but when she does, he may feel threatened and anxious.

Given these realities, the sexually assertive woman has to make a choice. Does she go back to being passive, waiting for her telephone to ring or her lover to dictate the sexual agenda? If she does, she takes care of his insecurities and his need to be in control. She protects him from having to relate to an equal adult. This choice is supported by many of our cultural values. But what is the cost to the woman psychologically? The cost is resentment, low self-esteem, and sense of not being in charge of her own life—i.e., being a child psychologically.

If a man is threatened by the fact that a woman is sexually assertive, what does that say about his psychological makeup? Is this the kind of man who can foster and develop an intimate relationship? Probably not, unless he is willing to make some major changes in his basic outlook on life.

A little sexual assertiveness can help you see if the man you are involved with is one with whom you can form a long-term relationship—assuming that is your intention. You will probably have some lonely times, but I believe it is better to accept the loneliness than to violate your self-esteem to humor an insecure man.

Most couples I've known want the initiation of sex to be equally shared. But in reality this seldom happens. Ideally, the couple is flexible in this regard—one partner may initiate for a period of time, then the other partner takes over.

Making Your Sexual Needs Understood

One of the biggest problems couples have when it comes to initiating sex is clear communication. Often they signal their desire to be sexual through a sort of code or by the use of innuendo. Perhaps one of them says, "I think I'll go upstairs and take a shower." Now this could mean that the person wants to get clean because he feels dirty, or it could mean that he is going to get clean because he wants to have sex. How is his partner to know? It's all guesswork. A response might be, "I'll be there in a few minutes." This could be interpreted as a yes to being sexual or as a statement that the partner is tired and just wants to go to sleep.

The stereotypical response of the woman who isn't interested in being sexual is, "I have a headache." Of course, the man could answer by saying "Well, take some aspirin and I'll wait twenty minutes." However, what the woman is probably really trying to convey is a flat no. But who knows?

To avoid disappointment, frustration, or hurt when asserting a sexual interest, communicate clearly. Express yourself in such a way that your partner knows exactly what you have in mind. You don't have to be crude—unless that is something that you and your partner like. Also, clarity doesn't have to be unromantic or clinical. When you express yourself clearly, the odds of getting what you want increase greatly. There are still no guarantees, though—sorry!

Another benefit of clarity when it comes to sexual communication is that it prevents or reduces the level of sexual assumptions. Since it is difficult for many couples in this culture to talk openly about sex, they tend to operate on unspoken assumptions. They assume what their partner likes or doesn't like what they want to do or don't want to do. Sometimes their assumptions may be correct, other times they may be way off base. For me, a sexual relationship is too sensitive and emotional—and important—to leave to guesswork.

Once I worked with a couple who both thought that the other didn't enjoy oral sexual stimulation. They developed this assumption early in their relationship. By the time I saw them as clients they had been married for eight years. One day in my office they discovered, through my questions, that they had misinterpreted one another's reactions during one of their earliest sexual encounters. Because they had built the assumption into their subsequent lovemaking, and had never communicated verbally about their preferences, they had lived together for almost a decade avoiding oral sex. They were both extremely surprised to discover oral sex high on the other partner's preference list. The lack of clear communication can distort a sexual relationship for a lifetime.

Structuring Time for Intimacy

Some couples ritualize their initiation of sexual activity. They develop an understanding that at a certain time they are supposed to become sexually involved—for example, Saturday night is sex night. Both partners have now succeeded in avoiding the emotional risk of initiating sex.

Unfortunately, eliminating risk also guarantees predictability. Without spontaneity, sex becomes routine and boring. And if the pre-arranged time for sex rolls around and one of the partners isn't interested, the routine is disrupted. To re-start the sexual relationship, one of the partners must now take the risk of initiating sex. If neither is willing to do so, much time may pass before they become sexually involved again. This sort of ritualization of sexual initiation often has an adverse effect on sexual frequency.

In some respects, planning in advance or structuring time for intimacy is necessary in order to maintain a long-term love relationship. This is especially true if the couple have small children. All too often I see couples who spend little if any quality time together without children, relatives, or friends.

With all the demands on their time, it becomes imperative that such couples deliberately set aside occasions for intimacy. When the time comes, they do not necessarily have to be physically sexual unless that is something they mutually want to do. But it is important that they have time to be intimate in the sense of being able to talk to one another about their inner thoughts and feelings, and about the important things occurring in their lives. It is essential that they be able to communicate in this way without being interrupted by children walking in and begging for attention, or having the phone ringing, or the television distracting their attention. This intimate time together on a regular basis is a necessary precursor to high quality sexual activity in the bedroom.

Sex and Spontaneity

On the other end of the spectrum from those couples who ritualize their sexual involvement, there are those who feel that sexual initiation should always occur spontaneously. They believe that sex shouldn't require them to make plans ahead of time—it should just happen naturally, like spontaneous combustion. It just happens whenever the urge hits, no matter when or where.

Now there's certainly nothing wrong with spontaneity. On the contrary! But for busy people and people with children, spontaneity as a prerequisite for sex doesn't always work. It is hard to be spontaneous with children running in and out of the bedroom—or any other room, for that matter. Somehow, children have an intuitive sense of when their parents are being sexual, and they love to cry or to come and say hello at that very time.

The only time that many couples with children can truly be spontaneous is when they are on a vacation without the children, staying in a hotel or motel. There, all they have is a room, a bed, and a television—which hopefully is off. In this sort of environment, spontaneous combustion is much more likely to take place.

Why Do We Initiate Sex?

Often when I'm working with a person who has a lack of interest in sex, the issue of sexual initiation is a concern as well. It is not difficult to see why sexual interest and the ability to initiate sex are related. But just how are they related? What motivates a person to initiate sexual activity?

Most clients, when asked what motivates them to have sex, usually say, "I just feel like it," or "It happens when I'm in the mood." They regard initiation as something you just don't think about—you just do it. But when someone isn't initiating or participating sexually, then it becomes something we need to look at closely.

Probably the idea that sexual initiation is unpremeditated goes back to the formative period of the sexual relationship. In the beginning, the desire for sexual activity isn't an issue; it's just a matter of when and where. At this phase, interest is primarily physiologically based. One or both partners are "turned on" sexually by the excitement, mystery, and newness of their developing relationship.

After a period of time, the newness of the other's body wears off. Both may still be quite attracted to each other physically, but there perhaps isn't the same almost instantaneous response there once was to seeing each other naked. This is a normal pattern in long-term relationships.

But a problem arises if the couple's motivation for sex is limited to physiology—in other words, if they don't initiate or participate in sexual activity unless they are feeling "horny" or sexually aroused. Gradually their relationship changes, to the point where they only feel the physiological urge perhaps twice a month. Their sexual frequency becomes limited to the infrequent times during which their hormones are in the right phase.

Now there is nothing wrong with initiating sex when the physiological urge motivates you; the problem is when you limit your sexual expression to those times only. What I propose to couples who find themselves in this predicament is that they add psychological motivators, which are not dependent on hormones, to their criteria for arousal.

The first of these psychological motivators is the good old Freudian pleasure principle. Simply put, this states that we keep on doing things from which we derive pleasure. If at this moment you were to think about eating ice cream, then if you like ice cream and are not on a diet, you probably would say "That sounds good—let's go!" This same principle holds true for sex. If I think about making love to my wife, it usually equates with pleasure, because that's what I experienced the last time we were involved sexually. So, why wouldn't I want to experience that pleasure again? Pleasure has a carry-over effect.

The second psychological motivater derives from the fundamental symbolic meaning of sexual interaction in a loving relationship. Sex represents the expression of love. It is a gift of love. It is a way to bond or connect in a very intimate way. Of course, sexual expression doesn't always represent a loving expression; it can be a purely physical act done for self-pleasure. As singer Tina Turner said in a past hit, "What's love got to do with it?" But for most couples in this Western culture, sexual intercourse represents the primary way to express their love for one another.

These two motivators—doing it because it felt pleasurable the last time, and because it is a way to express love—are ideally available to a couple every time they are in a sexually conducive environment. But these two motivators can be blocked or inhibited as motivation for sexual interaction.

What Inhibits Sexual Motivation?

What if your experience wasn't pleasant the last time you had sex? What if it was frustrating, disappointing, or anxiety-producing? You might be somewhat hesitant or cautious about initiating sexual activity. Perhaps the last time a man had intercourse he lost his erection. After that, he may be less inclined to initiate sexual activity with his partner in order to avoid the embarrassment of feeling inadequate again.

I often see women who aren't interested in initiating sex with their partners because they do not experience orgasm. They get pleasure from being close and being touched, but after a while the frustration of not experiencing an orgasm outweighs this pleasure. So just as the carry-over effect can be a motivator, it can also be an inhibitor.

The second psychological motivator for initiating sexual activity—its meaning as an expression of love or as a way of bonding intimately—can also be inhibited. What if you and your spouse have been arguing all day and you have resentments that have not been resolved? You are not going to feel much like giving gifts of love when you go to bed at night.

So while the two psychological motivators for sexual initiation are available to a couple every night, they can also be inhibited or blocked. When a couple go to bed at night and they are both sexually available (i.e., neither is tired to the point of losing consciousness or physically sick) and sex is initiated by one partner and the other isn't interested, this is cause for concern. I'm not concerned about them not having sex; I'm concerned because the conditions in which sex occurs have not been nurtured.

Generally, when this situation arises, they don't communicate much about it. They both ignore the fact that something is wrong, kiss good night, and go to sleep.

I would like to invent a device—a sort of Intimacy Avoidance Detector—that would go over a couple's headboard in their bedroom. When they go to sleep not feeling intimate enough with each other to be sexual if they wanted to be, the device would make a loud noise. The alarm wouldn't stop until they had re-established emotional intimacy.

So many couples who come to me don't see the many warning signals. Day after day goes by with both of them just going through the motions of everyday life, without making any real intimate connection with each other. They don't talk intimately, they are not very affectionate, and they're not very sexual. They are simply roommates. If this condition lasts for very long, irreparable damage can occur to the lover relationship.

The two psychological motivators are essential to keeping sexual activity frequent in a long-term relationship. They need tending and attention; nature takes care of the rest.

When your partner initiates, if you are interested in some type of sexual activity, then say yes by either participating in your partner's advances or by asserting your own desires. Remember that sexual activity may not include sexual intercourse. If you are not interested in sexual involvement, I recommend saying no, except for maybe a kiss and hug goodnight.

Some people, instead of saying no, play a little game with each other. Women tend to play this game more often because it is usually the man who is making the advances. The game goes like this:

"Honey, let's make love."

"No, I don't feel like it."

"Oh come on Honey, it would be fun."

"No, I'm tired."

"Ah, come on."

"Okay. If that's what will make you happy."

This little verbal game can have very destructive consequences on the couple's sexual communication. The credibility of the partner who says no is lost. The initiator doesn't know what to believe when it comes to the other's sexual interest. Even when the other does say yes, there will still be a question. This wondering—a mental activity—will get in the way of deep physical involvement. So if you want to be sexual, say yes—if not, say no and stick to it. It's that simple.

What to Do When Your Desires Aren't Clear

Our sexual desires are not always clear. Most of the time I find myself in the gray area, or neutral, as to my sexual desires. Many of my clients, when approached by their lovers while in this neutral sexual state, decline, saying they aren't in the mood.

What does it mean to be in a sexual mood? Does this mean that you have to be "horny" or sexually aroused? I think for a lot of people the answer is yes. In order for many people to be sexually involved, they feel they must be sexually aroused at the outset. This attitude is extremely limiting to a couple's sexual frequency and the amount of sexual pleasure in their life. An alternative attitude would be to *lend yourself to the experience* when you are feeling sexually neutral.

Let's say I have been working all day and I come home and my wife asserts herself by saying, "Dan, let's go upstairs and fool around." At that point sex may be the last thing on my mind. So what is my answer? If I base my answer on the old black-and-white idea, then the answer will be, "No, Honey, I'm not in the mood." If I base the answer on an attitude of openness, then I will say, "Sure, that sounds great, let's go upstairs." What I'm doing is lending myself to a sexual experience to see what happens. And of course, once I do lend myself to the experience the chances are excellent that I'll become sexually aroused.

In lending myself to the sexual experience, there is an important understanding that exists. That understanding is that just because I become sexually involved doesn't necessarily mean that I'm going all the way to having intercourse or an orgasm. If there is pressure to go all the way sexually, then I won't want to be involved, because I may only want to just hold and touch and not have intercourse. When the pressure doesn't exist, I often will want to go all the way.

Does this mean that we can't say no to our partner's sexual advances? We are drawing an important distinction here—especially for women. Remember, in the Victorian period sex was one of the wifely duties. She couldn't say no. But men have difficulty with this issue as well. We're told a "real man" always wants sex and is always ready to have it. So if a man were to say no, he wouldn't be living up to this false image of masculinity.

If a woman or a man is being involved sexually without really wanting to be, that person will consciously or unconsciously resent what is happening. This resentment builds and collects over a period of time and contaminates the couple's relationship to the point that one or both partners will turn off to sex and eventually to the marriage as well. What may seem like a gift at the moment may be a curse in the long run. So if you're feeling neutral, you might try lending yourself to the experience. But if you definitely do not want to participate, just say no.

The Fear of Rejection

For everyone—teenagers or adults, married people or singles—sexual initiation raises the fear of rejection. And for many of us this fear gets in the way of initiating sexual activity. The lower an individual's confidence or self-esteem, the more this becomes an issue.

To be turned down for sex, even in marriage, is a blow to the ego. To protect ourselves, we wait for the other person to make the first move. Fear of rejection is particularly anxiety-producing for men, because it is they who are usually expected to make the first move, and they who most often run the risk of being turned down.

I am reminded of my first dating experiences. Being a male, I was expected to ask the girl out for a date. I had to make that phone call. This, in a way, was the beginning of my sexual initiation. By asking that girl for a date, I was putting my neck on the chopping block. Without knowing it, she had the power to decide my worth relative to the opposite sex—I gave her that power. My ego hung in the balance.

She said no, and I felt rejected. At that time, I didn't know that her parents didn't want her dating. I went away feeling worthless. I'm sure that from the girl's perspective, she would have felt the same sense of rejection had she not been asked out on a date.

Was I really being rejected in this situation? In the world of single adult dating, this fear of rejection comes up all the time. If you go to a bar and ask a woman to dance and she says no, is she rejecting you? If you ask another woman for her phone number and she says no, is she rejecting you? If you ask another woman to go home with you for some late night activity and she says no, is she rejecting you? The answer to all these questions is no. You are not being rejected, even though it may feel that way.

Here's why. In the scene above, what the woman is saying no to is what the man wants—his agenda. The interaction happened so quickly that she can't possibly have gotten to know him in a meaningful way. She doesn't know his values, personality traits, or interests, since to get to know someone at this level takes time. Most single encounters don't involve that kind of time. So she simply doesn't know enough to reject him as a person, even though she may reject his agenda after a very superficial scrutiny. Even though this knowledge may still not make him feel great about being rebuffed, at least his self-esteem need not be in the gutter.

Let's look at a rejection in a long-term relationship. Suppose that I am being assertive. I clearly express to my wife my desire to have sex with her and she says, "No, not tonight, Dan. I'm just bushed." Is she rejecting me sexually? Again, the answer is no.

In this case my wife isn't rejecting me; she is just saying no to what I want. We have conflicting agendas: I want to make love, she wants to sleep. Both agendas are legitimate, but they're in conflict. So, I'm not being rejected, I'm merely disappointed in that I'm not getting what I want. I may be frustrated, but not rejected.

For my wife to reject me sexually, she would have to say something like, "No, not tonight or ever, Dan, because you are a sexual pervert, fat and ugly—and one of the most disgusting human beings I've ever met!" Now that's personal rejection!

If she keeps saying no to my sexual advances, after a while I'm going to wonder what the underlying reason is. But even when I see a couple where one of them has been saying no to the other's advances, she or he is usually not rejecting the other as a sexual partner. Usually, she or he is simply not feeling intimate enough outside the bedroom to be sexually involved. Or that partner might be feeling inadequate about his or her own abilities sexually, and thus afraid to be sexually involved. In either case, this has little to do with sexual rejection of the partner as a lover. I hope that with an understanding of the difference between sexual rejection and disappointment it will be easier for you to assert yourself sexually in whatever kind of personal relationship you may be involved.

Creating a Context for Intimacy

The last aspect of sexual initiation I would like to address involves setting the scene, that is, sexuality beyond what you do physically in bed. The idea of setting the scene first arises when couples begin dating. The goal is to make the other person want to be with you in an intimate way. For men, the idea often is to make the conquest, and their goal-oriented sexual world may include a "seduction den." Sexual seduction requires lots of effort, advance planning, and preparation.

When I knew I had a date with someone I really cared about, I would make sure that everything would go smoothly. Reservations were made for that special romantic restaurant, including the right table with the best location. I made sure that my car was clean, and that my house and bedroom were clean and neat. I chose appropriate clothes for the evening. Once back at my place, I lit a fire and candles, and put on some mellow background music. The scene was set.

Why did I put so much energy into trying to make the evening special? One goal was to get her in a sexy and romantic mood so that she would want to go to bed with me. Another goal was to show her how much I cared about her by putting out such an effort. If I were going over to a woman's house for dinner, I might experience the same type of evening.

There is nothing wrong with any of this. But a problem may occur when the "goal" has been achieved—when the conquest has been made or the commitment to the relationship has been established. The motivation is no longer present. The attitude becomes, "Let's just get it on and jump into the sack. Let's stop wasting our time with this preliminary stuff." We looked at this "meat and potatoes" attitude toward sex in chapter two. It opens the door to complacency and to taking the significant other for granted. It is particularly dangerous for couples who have been married for a few years.

I'm not saying that every time you plan to be sexually involved with your lover/spouse you have to spend four hours creating a romantic mood and environment. But you should consider doing so more than twice a year—on your anniversary and on Valentine's day!

Creating a sexual/romantic mood is especially important for couples with small children. It's hard to put yourself into a lover's frame of mind when you have diapers and kids' toys everywhere.

So it becomes essential for the couple to create some kind of refuge within their house where they can be alone. What is even more important than having a refuge is having a lovers' consciousness—looking at each other as a woman and man as opposed to just a wife and husband, or mother and father.

Creating Romance in a Long-Term Relationship

How can a couple stop taking their sexual relationship for granted? Once the goal of the conquest has been achieved, they need something to take its place. I went though a long personal journey of discovering how to maintain sexual attraction throughout the course of a committed relationship.

It was after I was married and had children that the idea of maintaining a lover's consciousness became a high priority in my life. My clients kept telling me that my ideas sounded great on paper, but with the reality of marriage and children I would see that they were too idealistic to be practical. They wanted me to agree with them that marriage and children inevitably drive your love life down the tubes. What more could one expect?

My wife and I have been married fourteen years now, and experience has taught me that it is possible to maintain a high quality love relationship with a spouse. The key is the motivation and ability to create this kind of relationship in the context of marriage.

I learned some valuable lessons about this from a roommate I had when I was single. He managed a local restaurant, and I thought he would be a great contact through which to meet the women who worked for him.

He was an expert at creating sexual ambiance. When he first moved into the apartment we shared, he went to work on his bedroom. He started decorating it in the way I would decorate a living room. He put in attractive, comfortable chairs, a fish tank, ferns, a little stereo, and he hung decorative rugs on the wall. His bedroom was a very comfortable place in which to relax.

Down the hall was my bedroom, devoid of warmth and comfort, more like a motel than a place where one person was living. There was a bed, a dresser, and a single picture on the wall. Guess whose room most people chose to be in? At the time, I was waiting for a woman who would come into my life and decorate my room. It was as if I had no sensuality or softness in my personality. When a woman did try to fill this void, I would feel uncomfortable. Women who didn't want to be my mother, of course, didn't want to have anything to do with me.

What I learned from this experience was that I needed to take the responsibility to fill that void in myself, as my roommate had done for himself, if I was going to be sexually attractive to mature women.

Another lesson I learned from my roommate had to do with the shape my body was in and the type of clothes I wore. I had never really thought much about my body shape in terms of its sexual appeal. I never watched what I ate or how much physical exercise I was getting. Of course, a woman's physical body shape made a big difference to me. Men were always checking women out with that "meat market" mentality. I had never heard about women looking at men in the same way. Of course they did, but I just hadn't heard about it.

My roommate began to alert me to the fact that women also like to look, and they are aroused by the way a man is physically built. They like men with cute rear ends and flat stomachs, although they may not be as vocal about their preferences as men are. Women in this culture have always been concerned about the way their bodies looked. It hasn't really been until recently that men acquired the same concern.

I started running and playing tennis. Instead of trying to win tournaments and medals, I participated in order to make myself feel good about my body. This raised my sexual self-esteem. While

I don't advocate extremes of self-indulgence and narcissism, I believe that each person can find a happy medium between physical narcissism and being a pot-bellied couch potato. I saw my double standard when it came to clothes. What my date wore made a major difference to my level of sexual attraction to her; yet I didn't care what I wore as long as I was clean and neat. I had come out of the sixties counterculture, and I had no regard for fashion unless it was anti-fashion. My roommate made me aware of the role that my clothes played in terms of my sexuality. When I put on my first pair of Calvins, I knew that I was making a sexual statement. In physical and metaphorical terms, I tossed out my faded Levis with their holes and patches.

Treating Love as though It Matters

When I was dating and going to meet a girlfriend, I would be very conscious of the casual clothes I chose. When I was married, I became aware of a trap that many married men fall into. When I went to work, I wore the nicest clothes I owned. At home, I wore my comfortable worst. While there's nothing wrong with comfort, in my case it represented the great enemy of a lover relationship—complacency—creeping in.

Why is it that once we are married, we lose this concern? We begin to think that marriage is forever, and that our spouse will always be there. If you begin to take your partner for granted, you are guaranteeing trouble for the relationship.

When couples separate after being married for a number of years, the way they relate to each other changes. Usually the one who had most often taken the other for granted while they were married now becomes frantic to get that spouse to let them resume living together. In my experience, it's usually the husband who has taken his wife for granted. Now he becomes a new courting lover, just as he may have been in the beginning of their relationship. He creates romantic weekend getaways, sends flowers, and tells his wife how much he loves her in person and by cards.

It is not uncommon, also, for someone who is separated and not interested in getting back with his or her spouse (at least right away) to make personal changes, all having to do with sexuality—losing weight, buying a new wardrobe, and perhaps buying a new sports car. It's as if this person could not let his or her sexuality out within the marital context.

Why do we have to be separate or single in order to keep our sexuality alive? Is it because we can't handle monogamy? Are we afraid that if we maintain an ongoing sexuality we will attract the opposite sex, and yield to temptation?

Men and women who downplay their sexuality by perhaps gaining weight or dressing like slobs may be trying to control their relationship by subconsciously denying a basic part of their identity—their sexuality. Usually they don't feel confident about the quality of the relationship or their own commitment to it. The more the relationship lacks in intimacy and love, the more this pattern takes over.

Whenever someone tries to control an intimate relationship in this way, their efforts often backfire and destroy the relationship. They trap themselves by denying full sexuality to themselves. They deny their spouse a sexual partner. The marriage becomes a self-created prison, from which either party is glad to escape.

Making an effort to keep romance in your long-term relationship pays off handsomely. Romance, as well as being pleasant in and of itself, is a terrific relationship-builder. As Alan and Donna Brauer put it in their book *ESO*, "If you think romance is a waste of time, think again. Paying attention to romance will win your romantic partner's warm attention in return. Isn't that what you want?"

Romance and sex—these are words that naturally go together. As we have seen, sexuality has to do with the way we communicate, the way we deal with conflicts, and the way we spend time together. When you are with a lover, you are not in bed all the time; you spend time together walking on the beach or having a picnic in the countryside, or sharing time together in some other way that you both enjoy. All of these are opportunities for romance, and for nurturing the lover aspect of your relationship. None of this has to change just because a commitment has been made, or because you are married.

Motivating Yourself to Love

How do you motivate yourself to maintain a lover's consciousness in a long-term, intimate relationship? When people come to me with this question, I try to help them see the rewards that will come from exerting the extra energy it takes. Usually if I tell them that they should do this because it will improve their relationship, they hear the logic, but their motivation only lasts about a week and then they go back to their old, complacent ways.

The key is motivation, and your primary motivation for cultivating your own lover attitude must be your own pleasure. If you are merely trying to make your partner happy, seeing sex as an obligation, then your efforts will come to nothing. You will make your partner happy if you put energy into your relationship because it makes you feel good.

A second motivation for nurturing your lover relationship—and a very real one—is fear of losing your lover because of neglect. She or he might have an affair. It is naive to think that your wife just takes care of the kids at home, or that your husband is too busy and he's just not that type of guy. If you are not treating your spouse like a lover, then some very important emotional needs are not being fulfilled. The likelihood of there being an affair increases dramatically, if either partner has much self-esteem. I know that this sounds harsh, but that's the reality in today's world.

Both of these motivations arise from a core desire that I am assuming you have—the desire for a lover. If that is not what you want—if your relationship is just a game, or a strategy for staving off insecurity—then you and your partner need to know that. But if you do in fact want a passionate, exciting, and pleasurable relationship, then you can have what you want—if you are willing to invest some time and effort in the ways we've considered in this chapter.

Sexual initiation is much more than what you do in the bedroom. It has to do with how much you are willing to acknowledge your own and your partner's sexuality. You do this by understanding that you do not have to be limited to rigid rules of initiation that society has taught. You do it by recognizing that spontaneity sometimes needs a little assistance. You do it by learning to communicate honestly and openly about what you want sexually. You do it by not taking your partner for granted. And you do it by remembering that the romance that makes any relationship exciting needs a bit of nurturing from time to time.

How Often Is Normal?

One of the questions I am most frequently asked is, "How often is it normal for a couple to make love? Is it once a week, every day, three times a day, or once a month?"

Of course, there are statistics that would seem to answer this question. But I am not going to cite those statistics here, because to do so would only serve to further concretize the assumptions that are built into the question. I try to stay away from any discussion about "What is normal?" and I suggest that couples do the same, since whatever statistics come to mind tend merely to be used as ammunition for debate.

A frequency problem exists not when a couple deviates from some statistical norm, but when there is a significant discrepancy between the desires of the two people—when, for example, one partner wants to make love once a week, while the other wants to do so once a month. That's a frequency problem. If, on the other hand, both partners are content with being sexually involved once a month, then who is to say that they have a problem?

Presently, of all the sexual problems that I encounter, sexual frequency is the most common. One reason for this is the fact that in recent years, for the first time, it has become acceptable for women to want more sexual frequency within their marriage, so they are less willing to accept a limited sex life than they might have been in the past.

This may be uncomfortable for husbands who are accustomed to being in the controlling position, at least with regard to sexual initiation. They may perceive their wives' increased interest as pressure on them to perform, which in turn may intimidate them and cause them to become less interested in sex. The outcome, often, is reduced frequency.

Sex as a Measure of Emotional Intimacy

Another reason for problems with sexual frequency is a lack of emotional intimacy in the relationship. If a couple are not close emotionally, they can cover up the fact by appearing to be good parents, friends, and social partners. From the outside—and perhaps even to themselves—they appear to be a happy couple. But the appearance is only superficial. One thing they can't cover up is what happens in the bedroom—which is usually very little. In their case, lack of sexual frequency becomes the problem. It is easier for them to identify this obvious symptom as their problem than it is for them to talk about the cause, which is lack of emotional intimacy in their marriage.

Often couples who feel they have a problem with frequency will try to increase their sexual desire. One method I'm seeing used increasingly these days is the viewing of X-rated films rented from the local video store. The couple's intent is that by watching other people in very explicit sexual activity, they will become aroused themselves so that then they will want to make love. Now I have nothing against watching X-rated films, but I don't believe any couple should rely on this method. If they do, the chances are very good that the real problem is that the couple involved is not close enough to want to be sexual without the presence of explicit, visual erotic stimulation.

Some people try to increase their sexual frequency by using drugs and alcohol. Marijuana particularly is used to temporarily remove blocks to emotional closeness, so that the couple can then be physically close. It represses the hurt and anger that have built up over the years to inhibit sexual response and desire. If the only way a couple can successfully engage in sexual activity is through the use of drugs, their actual problem is probably a lack of emotional intimacy.

Women's Headaches or Men's Headaches?

Generally, when the subject of sexual frequency comes up for discussion, most people assume that it is the woman who isn't interested in sex. After all, she is always the one depicted in the popular media as having a headache. In my clinical experience, however, I find this not the case. In fact, it seems that I see many more men who lack sexual interest. Women seldom tell me that they are not interested in sex. But they often say that in order to have physical intimacy, they first need to have some kind of personal dialogue that allows them to feel close.

This brings up a basic conflict in the sexual programming we receive from our culture. Generally, women are given the message when they are children that in order to be sexually involved with a man a woman should have deep feelings for him, or that she should be in a committed relationship. Even if a woman has sex for sex's sake, a certain amount of guilt and self-condemnation may go with the momentary pleasure. Talking about emotions and spending intimate time together outside the bedroom are important prerequisites to sex for most women.

Contrast this to the sexual programming that men receive in this culture. They are told in many ways that it's not masculine to express emotions (other than anger) verbally, and that the only way for a man to make intimate contact with a woman is through sexual intercourse.

In many relationships the very different teachings of men and women in our society produce an emotional standoff for couples. The husband says, "Let's make love," and the wife says, "Not until I feel closer to you emotionally." But the man cannot allow himself to become emotionally closer in the way that the woman needs except through sex, since to do so would imply that he was less of a man. An impasse is created and sexual frequency between the couple drops off radically.

Frigidity

Typically, when a woman's sexual interest is gone, or has diminished, either she or her lover will use the word "frigid" to describe her behavior. I don't like this word because it implies an incurable disease or a permanent character trait. There isn't much she can do about it; she is just a frigid person. The term "frigidity" is confusing, and I recommend that it be discarded. It presently is used to refer to women who experience a range of sexual response, from total lack of erotic feelings to minor degrees of orgasmic inhibition. The word seems to imply coldness and hostility toward men. The fact is that women who suffer from sexual dysfunctions are frequently warm and responsive.

Interestingly, you never hear about frigid men. Why is this? I see as many men who lack real desire as I do women, but they don't walk into my office having been labelled frigid. To me, this is a clue to the sexist mentality of the label-makers.

The label of frigidity tends to blind people to the real cause of their problems. Behind the so-called frigid woman's lack of sexual desire is usually a great deal of repressed anger and hurt.

I see the so-called sexually frigid woman (metaphorically) as a nuclear reactor. As her feelings of resentment and anger became repressed, she starts to build a concrete wall around them, like the containment wall of a reactor building. Inside are the radioactive materials that mustn't be allowed to escape to contaminate the environment.

This is how the frigid woman feels: inside there is anger that must not be expressed; and the more anger, the thicker the wall. The outside of the reactor building might feel cold, but inside is a hot core of radioactive material.

The irony is that the frigid woman often builds this wall to protect her marriage. She is afraid that if she expresses her resentments it will alienate her lover. Actually the opposite is true, because as she turns off her anger, she also blocks her sexuality, which in the end will truly alienate her lover and probably end the relationship she is trying to preserve.

Some Common Blocks to Sexual Desire

The most common inhibitor of sexual desire is repressed anger, or anger that is ineffectively communicated in the moment. Generally when there is a lack of sexual frequency, built-up resentments are the cause. It is very difficult to be intimate or sexually turned on with your lover if you are angry. Nobody is going to be able to enjoy intimacy and sexual closeness until the anger has been dealt with.

Unfortunately, many people are uncomfortable expressing or receiving anger, and so rather than dealing with it, they ignore or repress it. It doesn't matter whether a resentment is little or big, old or new. When you block the anger or don't acknowledge and listen to it, then you might as well forget about being lovers.

One of the first things I told my wife when we were married was, "If I do anything that you resent, whether it's tiny or huge, I want you to tell me right away." Before I learned this lesson, my attitude had been, "Don't bug me about the little things. I have enough to worry about without having to deal with your petty resentments and complaints." I was telling my partner to stifle or suppress her anger.

This latter attitude is a sure-fire way to turn off your lover's sexual desire. Indeed, this effect is so predictable that when I hear someone complain about the lack of sex in a relationship, I assume that the real problem is probably suppressed anger.

When I told my wife to express her resentments and not to hold anything back, she was a little shocked. At first she didn't believe me. She replied, "You want me to complain and to bug you? Won't you think I'm just being bitchy? You must either be crazy or some kind of masochist." But when I told her my reasoning, she understood. I said that while I don't enjoy hearing her resentments, I know that if she expresses them rather than holding them back she will be as sexually responsive to me on our twenty-fifth wedding anniversary as she was at the beginning of our marriage.

The same principle holds true in the dating world. Often I'm told, "You know, Dan, my sexual relationships start off being so exciting but after a month or so they just become humdrum; I don't understand why." My response is that after a couple spend some time together they start to irritate each other with specific behaviors. It is only natural for this to happen. Since they have just started dating, they usually don't want to express any resentments. They are overwhelmed by their positive feelings for one another, and they begin to block the negative ones. After a month or so, this blocking process begins to take its toll on the couple's sexual responsiveness, both in and out of bed.

Most single people who find themselves in this situation write it off to boredom with the relationship. They decide it is time to move on to another person. They never seem to realize why the pattern of excitement followed by boredom keeps repeating itself. When this happens to a married couple, they can't so easily move on to another relationship, so they find other things to occupy their interest.

Anger and Desire

The most common source of anger in long-term relationships is a power struggle between the partners. The subject of the power struggle really isn't important, except that it might have some effect on the intensity of the anger. What is important is that the partners are in a contest over control of something in their relationship.

When this occurs, they become adversaries. As Helen Singer Kaplan states, "Regardless of the origin of anger, it is not possible for most persons to feel sexual desire for the enemy. Anger and love act as mutual inhibitants." Partners involved in a power struggle give up their need to be close and intimate because they don't really want the intimacy; they would rather win the battle. But even if they win the battle, they lose the relationship, at least in terms of being lovers.

As we have seen, quality sex requires vulnerability. If a couple are competing for control, the last thing they want to do is to lower their defenses and abandon themselves to sexual pleasure; instead, it is safer to block their feelings of sexual desire.

Some couples report to me that after they get angry with each other, yelling and calling each other names, they start to have sexual feelings toward each other. Often these feelings lead to a very satisfying sexual experience. This happens for several reasons. One is that they have probably released anger that was previously repressed; it was getting in the way of their sexual desire. That's why couples who do a great deal of vocalizing about their resentments tend to have greater sexual frequency in their marriage than couples who never fight.

I don't want to suggest that in order to have a high frequency of sexual activity in a marriage you should yell and scream at each other. On the contrary. It is good to express your resentments and anger with your partner, but do so in a constructive manner, preferably using "I" messages as opposed to "you" messages. For example, "I am angry that you didn't pick up the theater tickets," rather than, "You are inconsiderate and lazy." The first, you'll note, lets the other person know how you feel. The second is an attack on the person's character. Expressing the former ultimately invites intimacy; the latter is one of the most powerful ways available for pushing another person away.

While yelling and screaming may work for the moment, releasing anger so that sexual desire many come to the surface, in the long run it may bury desire. This is because when a couple communicate in such a coarse, ineffective way they usually hurt each other in the process. Eventually this hurt will accumulate in emotional scar tissue—which blocks sexual desire.

Sometimes, when partners have expressed their anger aggressively, they want to be close because of fear. They are each afraid that, having yelled or called the other names, they have hurt their lover (and, of course, they have), and therefore the lover might leave or abandon them. As a way to compensate for this fear, they reach out and become sexually close. What better way to assuage these fears of abandonment than by having sexual intercourse? This pattern only happens if the fear of abandonment is experienced by both partners. It may work for a while, but eventually the pattern will break down because you can only hurt someone for so long before that person will stop wanting to be close. This will occur more rapidly as a person's self-esteem increases and, as a result, the fear of being abandoned or living alone decreases.

Anxiety inhibits sexual desire. As I mentioned earlier, the more a couple or individual *work* at a goal, the more anxiety they create for themselves. The more sexual anxiety they create, the less sexual pleasure they will experience. When the pleasure goes out of their sexual experience, then their motivation to participate sexually is lost. Sexual frequency diminishes.

It is essential to relax and let go in order to experience sexual pleasure. The sources of sexual anxiety are many, and these are in turn the cause of most of the the sexual dysfunctions that couples experience. We will look at these sources of anxiety later in the chapter on sexual dysfunctions.

Relationship Issues that Block Sex

As we saw in chapter three, emotional intimacy is the prerequisite for sexual frequency. When it is absent, sexual frequency drops off. Let's look briefly at other relationship issues that also affect a couple's sexual frequency.

The first issue is that of trust. There has to be a fundamental trust between partners for them to have a quality sexual relationship over an extended period of time. They have to trust that their partner/lover is not out to hurt them in any way; that their partner is committed to the relationship, meaning that their partner isn't contemplating leaving soon, or is sexually or emotionally involved with someone else; and that their partner will be there to give emotional support if they make themselves vulnerable and communicate their emotions. At the core of the matter is the trust that one is being accepted and that the atmosphere is free of judgment.

Trust has to do not only with trusting your partner, but with trusting yourself as well. You must be able to trust yourself to maintain your own sense of identity before you can become emotionally intimate with a lover. Otherwise you will tend to cave in or sell out on your needs or wants because you are afraid that you won't be loved if you create a conflict. Also, you must have trust or confidence in yourself that once you do become emotionally vulnerable, if the relationship becomes detrimental to your mental health you will be able to terminate the relationship.

Without trust in all its forms, emotional vulnerability as described in chapter three cannot flourish. Without vulnerability, sexual quality is usually poor, and as a consequence, sexual frequency drops off.

Earlier in this chapter we took a brief look at the subject of power struggles and competition for control. These constitute a another issue affecting a couple's sexual life.

Who is the boss? Who makes the decisions about what happens in the relationship? When a couple develop a competitive style of relating, their ability to maintain a lover relationship diminishes. In the struggle for power, sex can become either a weapon or a prize for barter—"If you do this for me, then maybe you might get some tonight." The person who thinks this way may be depriving his or her partner of sexual pleasure; at the same time that person is also losing.

Sacrificing your own sexual needs to get back at your partner for the moment makes both of you losers. You may win the battle, but in the end you will lose what was most important to you—the relationship itself.

Power struggles usually result from low self-esteem, which leads people to feel a need for control over their partner. Attempts to control may take many forms, from subtle to overt. A common type of power struggle has to do with one partner's weight problem and its impact on the couple's sexual frequency. Often the woman is overweight and her male partner exhibits a lack of sexual interest. His basic position might be stated, "If only you would lose weight," or "If only you weighed the same as when we first got married," or "If only you lost the weight you gained during your pregnancy, then I might be interested in making love." Her response might be to eat more as a way of getting back at him. But the heavier she gets, the more he becomes entrenched in his position. What results is a classic power struggle with intimacy and sexual frequency as its casualties.

When couples get married, they establish certain assumptions or agreements. Often these agreements are made unconsciously, tacitly, or in the mind of only one partner. Sometimes the agreements are tied to sex; for example, "If you support me in the lifestyle that I expect, then you can expect me to be there for you sexually," or "I will always want to make love to you as long as you are faithful; if you cheat on me, then forget about sex."

Many men unconsciously assume that they have an agreement with their wives that says, "You will never change and will always be the girl I married." If confronted, the man would probably deny having this assumption. But when his wife does change, he feels threatened and resentful, as if an agreement has been broken. As a result, he is not interested in being sexually intimate with her—though he may not consciously understand why. When these assumed agreements are not kept, sexual frequency within a marital relationship is impaired. But the reason for the breakdown is not at all apparent to the partners.

Another source of resentment that blocks sexual desire is a longing for romance—a desire for the close, loving attention that usually comes in the early stages of dating. Alan and Donna Brauer write, "When women are sexually frustrated and miss the positive romantic attention they feel they need, we've found they become withdrawn, depressed, or angry. In a word, irritable. This reaction, which is often unconscious, may lead them to start arguments over issues that are seemingly unrelated. That sounds irrational, but it operates by the logic of frustration: at least their arguing makes their partners pay attention, and better angry attention than none at all."

Regular romantic input and intimacy can go a long way toward reducing the level of frustration and resentment in the relationship. This needs to be a part of daily living—not just an awkward flourish on special occasions or an obligatory gesture just before bed.

Quality and Sexual Frequency

The basis of an active sexual relationship is the quality of the experience for the partners involved. Good quality means high sexual pleasure. When the amount of sexual pleasure drops off for either partner, then that partner loses interest. That's when sexual frequency becomes a problem.

Sexual quality suffers when one partner's sexual interest is very high, nearly insatiable, while the other's is almost nonexistent. Let's take the case of Sue and Jack. Jack seems to always want to make love, while Sue could take it or leave it. Like many couples who have the same problem, Sue and Jack follow a certain pattern, or scenario. It's as if they are following an unwritten script.

Usually Jack and Sue wait to have sex until late at night—when the kids have gone to sleep, all their chores are done, and their favorite television shows are over. If it is a weekday, they both have worked all day. They are tired. Still they have to get up early and get the kids ready to go to school and get themselves ready to go to work. They can't sleep in and have a leisurely morning together in bed.

When Sue and Jack get into bed together, Jack immediately wants to make love. In fact, from Sue's point of view, Jack's sex drive is insatiable—all he wants to do is make love. She, on the other hand, would probably like to do so once a month. Jack begins touching or grabbing her in the same way he does every night. Sue feels pressured to make love. She thinks, "If I don't have sex with him, he might go somewhere else. I do love him and he works so hard to support us. After all, it's my wifely duty." So, she usually consents to being sexual with Jack whether she wants to or not.

When they start interacting sexually, there is tension between them. They are not relaxed with each other. Jack senses Sue's hurry-up-and-get-it-over-with attitude, so he proceeds with a very goal-oriented style of touching, doing just enough so that it appears that Sue is ready to have intercourse. He focuses primarily on her breasts and genitals, with very little foreplay. Once she seems ready, Jack gets on top in the missionary position. He senses Sue's tension. Even though she is a good actress, the act eventually wears thin. As a result, Jack doesn't last long before ejaculating. He isn't able to relax and enjoy whatever sexual pleasure he is experiencing; all he is really able to do is relieve his sexual tension, just as he would if he were masturbating.

As for Sue, the experience provides little, if any, sexual pleasure. On occasions when she starts to get excited, he usually ejaculates before she can really get into the experience; so, after a while, she stops herself from becoming aroused. After he ejaculates, he rolls over and goes to sleep. She does get a pleasurable feeling being physically close to her husband for a period of time, and gives him a goodnight kiss. Sue may feel relieved that she has satisfied Jack for the moment, but the next night the whole process begins again.

As I said in our discussion of meat and potatoes sex, we're describing here a couple engaging in "junk-sex," from which they get as much real nourishment as they'd expect to get from eating burgers and fries at the local fast food restaurant every night. There may be nothing wrong with junk-food or junk-sex once in a while, but a steady diet of it is unhealthy and deadening to the palate. It also gets boring. When you've gotten a "quick fix" at the fast-food restaurant, you're satisfied for the moment, but several hours later you're hungry again. Doesn't this describe Jack's sexual experience?

Continuing the metaphor, my advice to Jack and Sue would be to stop the junk habit, save up their money, and choose an evening to go to the best "restaurant" in town. When you spend eighty or a hundred dollars for dinner, you're not going to gobble it up in fifteen minutes. You're much more likely to savor every bite.

How would this metaphor translate into Jack's and Sue's sexual relationship? If they were to take my advice, the following changes would take place: First, they would make love more slowly and leisurely. I'd say to Jack, "What's the hurry? Slow down. You should savor something so pleasurable." Second, they would spend more time touching—but without any goals. Both would begin to experience more pleasure.

As their sexual pleasure increases Jack and Sue's whole relationship changes. Jack's seemingly insatiable sex drive suddenly seems to have been satisfied. He stops pressuring Sue to be sexually involved every night. You might think that since their sexual relationship is now more pleasurable, he would want to have sex more often. But like a great and memorable dinner in a fine restaurant, sex becomes so satisfying that he no longer feels the constant need for "junk." Jack is being satisfied sexually in a way that his previous masturbatory style of relating could never never do for him. As his satisfaction increases, his seemingly insatiable activity decreases. Both he and Sue are becoming "sexual gourmets."

Sue's sexual interest increases with these changes. Now she starts initiating sexual activity, since Jack is no longer pressuring her every night. Jack's more relaxed posture gives Sue a chance to come on to him for a change. Also, there is more motivation for Sue to initiate sex with Jack, because she is getting more pleasure out of the experience. There is a great deal more touching, more foreplay, because Jack isn't in such a hurry now. The tension between them is gone because Sue is interested in being sexual, so Jack is now more relaxed sexually and doesn't ejaculate as fast when they have intercourse. This is another source of pleasure for Sue, and another motivation for her to be more involved sexually.

To summarize: as Jack and Sue develop their "tastes" for "gourmet sex," Jack lets go of his compulsive intensity where sex is concerned and Sue's sexual interest starts to increase. Over time, their desires will begin to balance. When the level of sexual pleasure in a relationship increases, sexual satisfaction stays high—but not at a level that would reflect insatiable desire on the part of either or both partners. Extreme frequency of sexual activity is generally the result either of people trying to play out their fantasies, or of the lack of real sexual quality or satisfaction in a relationship.

In the final analysis, questions of frequency generally give way to questions of quality. If there is quality in our experiences when we do have sex, we don't usually keep score, nor do we compulsively come back again and again, night after night, attempting to satisfy a misguided appetite. The most satisfying sexual relationships aren't like ball games where the person scoring the most points wins. They're more like vacations where goals are forgotten and there is time to savor the varied delights of the senses that deepen intimacy and erase the petty tension of daily life.

Discovering Your Whole Body
as One Big Sex Organ

The purpose of this chapter is to review certain aspects of human sexual physiology, knowledge of which can aid you in increasing the level of sexual pleasure in your relationship. The subject of physiology may, to some readers, imply something clinical or boring. I can assure that what we will be considering is far from boring. For the most part, we will be exploring the question, "What creates a sexual response?"

The Four Phases of Sexual Pleasure

Before 1954, when William Masters began his research, no one had ever studied human sexual behavior in the laboratory. Masters and Johnson's findings had a profound impact on the way we understand the human sexual response. One of their most important contributions was the discovery that the sexual response for both men and women occurs in four phases: excitement, the plateau, orgasm, and resolution.

The Excitement Phase. In this stage, the primary physiological event is "vasocongestion"—meaning, quite simply, an increased blood flow to specific parts of the body, primarily the genitals. In men, this produces an erect penis. In females, the most obvious change is increased moisture in the vagina. Also, the glans of the clitoris (the tip) swells, the breasts swell somewhat, and the nipples become erect. General effects for both sexes in the excitement phase include an increase in heart rate and blood pressure, and accelerated breathing.

The Plateau Phase. In this phase, vasocongestion reaches its peak. The penis is fully erect and the scrotum is pulled close to the body. A few drops of fluid are secreted by the Cowper's glands and appear at the head of the penis. This fluid may carry live sperm, even if the man has not yet ejaculated. This is why the withdrawal method of birth control is so ineffective.

For the woman, the plateau phase is characterized by the creation of the orgasmic platform. This is a swelling of the walls of the outer third of the vagina, which tends to reduce the size of the vaginal entrance. During intercourse, this gives the man the sensation of gripping at his penis.

The Orgasm Phase. For men, orgasm consists of a series of rhythmic contractions in the pelvis at 0.8-second intervals. For women, the rhythmic muscular contractions of orgasm occur at the same rate, but in her case there is usually no clear external sign that an orgasm has occurred.

For both men and women there are significant increases in pulse rate, blood pressure, and breathing rate during this stage. Muscles throughout the body, from the face to the toes, may contract.

The Resolution Phase. Here, the body returns essentially to its original, unaroused state. This phase generally takes from 15 to 30 minutes.

These stages do not necessarily occur in a fixed or rigid sequence that once set in motion proceeds in a straight line from beginning to end. A person can be at the plateau stage and move back to the excitement stage. Indeed, it is the awareness of—and the ability to work with—this flexibility (particularly on the part of the man) that allows the couple to maximize their sexual pleasure.

Generally, a man's sexual response pattern through the four stages is very predictable. He becomes excited, reaches a plateau, ejaculates, and passes back to resolution—at which point he kisses his wife, rolls over, and falls asleep. The amount of time spent at each phase varies, depending on the man's age and sexual experience. Women, on the other hand, usually have a much more varied path through the four stages. She may become excited and move to the plateau phase, then go back to excitement, then to plateau, and then finally peak into orgasm.

Some women, on the other hand, may move through the excitement phase to the plateau, stay there, have an orgasm, go back to plateau, and then have another orgasm. Women seem to be more flexible and more accepting of these variations than men.

There is no right or wrong way to respond through the four stages. What is important is to be flexible and responsive in the moment—a sure antidote to sexual boredom.

Often, the speed and intensity of a person's sexual response is mistaken for the intensity of pleasure he or she experiences. But the degree to which one sexual experience is better or more pleasurable than another depends on each individual's perspective and level of personal satisfaction.

Physiological Differences Between Women and Men

One of the physiological sexual differences between men and women is that men have what is called the "point of inevitability." This means that once a male reaches a certain level of sexual stimulation at the end of the plateau stage, he cannot stop his ejaculation from occurring. Women, on the other hand, have no point of inevitability. They can reach a high level of sexual stimulation right to the edge of orgasm and stop.

The knowledge of this fact can help a man experience more pleasure out of sex. When he becomes aware of getting close to his point of inevitability, a man can maintain his sexual response at the plateau stage, which increases the amount of sexual stimulation and therefore the amount of pleasure he can experience. In order to do this he and his partner must be flexible enough to shift stimulation away from the genitals so that the man's level of arousal decreases. This may include withdrawal during intercourse. All of this is also relevant to the problem of premature ejaculation, which we will consider in the next chapter.

Multiple Orgasm in Women— Unfortunately Not for Men

Prior to Masters and Johnson's research, it was believed that women's orgasms were similar to men's, in that after a woman experienced one orgasm, she entered a refractory period. The refractory period is the time that must pass following one orgasm before another is possible. Masters and Johnson found that the refractory period applies only to men. In other words, women have the physiological capacity to have one orgasm followed by another within a very short period of time. This is known as multiple orgasms. Men, unfortunately, have to wait out their refractory period—with the amount of time varying from one man to another. Physical health, nutrition, and the level of fatigue also play a part in the duration of the refractory period. Generally, the older the man, the longer the refractory period.

Masters and Johnson's research suggested that many women experience multiple orgasms, and that all women, if properly stimulated, have this physiological capacity. How many orgasms a woman can experience is up to her, depending on her level of satisfaction. Often a woman who can experience multiple orgasms may be satisfied with just one.

Usually, in order for a woman to experience multiple orgasms, she and her partner must be flexible enough to provide stimulation through oral or manual contact. This is because few men will last long enough during intercourse to bring a woman to another orgasm.

A note of caution: don't make multiple orgasms a sexual goal. If the man judges his performance by how many times he is able to bring his partner to orgasm, or if the woman is disappointed because she is able to have only two orgasms instead of five, then their sexual experience together loses spontaneity. It becomes work instead of pleasure.

Sexual Adequacy in Physiological Terms

In his article, "Sexual Adequacy in America," Philip Slater postulates that most men's criteria for sexual adequacy are not the same as most women's. A man's adequacy as a lover is usually thought to be determined by his ability to have an erection, whereas a woman's is thought to be determined by her orgasmic capacity. These criteria correspond with two different phases of the sexual response patterns—excitement and orgasm.

A man is also thought to be adequate if he is proficient at stimulating a woman to orgasm, preferably through the use of his penis; a "real man" doesn't need to use his hands or mouth. A woman is judged adequate to the degree that she is able to achieve an orgasm rapidly through vaginal intercourse. Also, a woman is defined as sexually adequate if she can make the man feel that he is sexually adequate—the impossible task!

If we summarize these common criteria for sexual adequacy, we arrive at the following: a man is adequate if he can delay orgasm, while a woman is adequate if she can accelerate orgasm. But in our culture, women's sexuality is often judged by the standards of the man's sexuality. This, of course, is a mistake. Why does the woman have to be in a hurry to have an orgasm? What's the rush? Why should a man's sexual response serve as the basis for assessing woman's sexual response?

Why shouldn't women serve as the standard of reference? In that case, few men would measure up. Indeed, Slater believes that the fairest and most useful definition of sexual adequacy is the ability to tolerate and sustain pleasurable stimulation without release. It is clear, by this definition, that women can absorb and tolerate more pleasure than men. But in our culture, many women have been made to feel inadequate for the very fact that they can relax and enjoy much sensuous pleasure and intimacy.

Often women complain that they take a long time to reach orgasm. Notwithstanding the possibility of inadequate stimulation by their partner, I say to them, "What is your hurry? Are you enjoying the experience along the way?" Usually, they respond with a definite yes. "Then what's the problem?" "My husband thinks that since I take a long time to have an orgasm, I might be frigid."

The truth is that each individual's sexuality is uniquely his or her own. We need to accept this uniqueness in ourselves and our partners.

Men, Slow Down!

All too many men are in a hurry, sexually speaking. They talk about sex as if it were the most important part of their daily lives, yet when they finally have the opportunity to be sexual, they rush to get it over with. Why? The answer lies partly in social conditioning. The man's social role as provider and defender leaves little space for relaxing and receiving. Slater states it this way: "Perhaps men have become sexually handicapped relative to women, not just in the physiological sense of having a finite capacity for repetition, but culturally, in the sense of having evolved a social role that limits their capacity for pleasure."

One seldom sees a television commercial for bath oils featuring a man luxuriating in a bubble bath. Why? Because few men take the time for a slow bath. They take quick showers, in and out. Many men find it difficult to just relax and experience the pleasure of the moment. They have to be producing, working, or achieving something. Relaxation has no goal and offers no obvious reward for the time spent. The more an individual cultivates a work/achievement mentality, the greater the negative effect it will have on his or her personal erotic life. Work and sex are natural enemies.

Another reason men seem to be in such a hurry sexually is that they are uncomfortable with the physical intimacy that prolonged sex creates. They are particularly uncomfortable with extended foreplay and touching.

This kind of loving involves much more vulnerability than the straight-ahead-wham-bam-thank-you-ma'am sort of sexual experience. Therefore men often find themselves in an emotional double bind. Part of them wants to be sexual, to enjoy all the pleasure they can, but another part fears intimacy and the experience of being psychologically or physically vulnerable. This double bind leads to the common male syndrome that we have already described—the watered-down, diluted, fast-food type of sexual experience, resulting in sexual malnutrition. Men who suffer from this syndrome never seem to get enough sex, because they are unable to really relax and enjoy the sexual experiences they already have.

Changing the Male Stereotype

Not all men are caught in this sexual trap, of course, but from my experience counseling couples I have to say that many are. There is, however, a way out. This requires reevaluating the masculine role that this culture has programmed into our consciousness. In other words, we have to develop new attitudes that make it okay to open ourselves up to pleasure for its own sake, without having to show something for the time spent.

Men need to understand their fear of vulnerability in order to overcome it. The most common form it takes is the fear of the loss of identity, of being overwhelmed by their partner. In the section on vulnerability in chapter three, I mentioned that it is essential for there to be trust between partners if vulnerability is to flourish. It is also important for a person to trust him- or herself. A man may trust his wife, believing that she isn't going to hurt him, but be afraid that he will lose himself if he becomes emotionally involved.

To enjoy intimate relationship we need the kind of self-confidence that allows an accomplished skier to abandon herself to the pull of gravity. We must trust ourselves that we can take care of our identity. Many men fear being dominated by women. This might be due to the fact that when they were little boys they had controlling mothers or a school teacher or a first love. But they were little boys then; now that they are grown adults they have a choice. Remember, no one can control or dominate us in an intimate relationship unless we allow them to do so; as adults, that choice is ours.

What Makes Up the Human Sexual Response?

Masters and Johnson's model of the sexual response cycle has been criticized for its omission of the psychological aspects of sexual response. Bernie Zilbergeld and Carol Ellison have stated that there are two essential components in the sexual response process—first, sexual desire and second, arousal.

The human sexual response is not an automatic, pushbutton event that occurs in the sexual organs. Some people believe that it is, and when their bodies don't operate this way they blame their bodies. They tend to look for simple solutions, as if taking a pill or getting a shot would solve everything. They look at their bodies as if they were pieces of machinery, ignoring the complexities involved.

The human sexual response is a multidimensional event. It is conditioned by several factors, including: emotions, thoughts, knowledge about sex (including what has been learned from past sexual experiences), and personal or cultural values relating to sexual behavior. These combined influences, along with our physiological responses, will determine our total sexual experience.

Given all the variables involved, the process is obviously not a simple or automatic one. Whether one is experienced or inexperienced, individual sexual response usually requires an extended set of thoughtful decisions.

When I was a very young man I labored under the misconception that touching a woman's nipples caused an automatic increase of blood flow to her genitals. My concept was that there were nerves running directly from the breasts to the genitals and thus to a specific erotic portion of the brain. If this "circuit" was turned on in any way, the woman was "turned on" sexually. It is this sort of misconception that leads many men to engage in what has been called "pushbutton" sex—meaning that all they have to do is touch a woman's breasts and then rub her genitals and that's it for foreplay.

As I became more sophisticated sexually I discovered that the nerve endings in my feet are the same as the nerve endings in my penis. In other words, there are no specialized nerve endings that transport sexual information to the brain. Nerve endings are like telephone cables—ignorant of content, just delivering raw information. When a physician stimulates the nerve endings in my genitals during an examination I don't experience a sexual response. However, if my wife stimulates the same nerve endings in a sexual context, I may have a very strong sexual response, depending on what I myself bring to that experience. The same nerve endings are being stimulated in both instances, but with very different results.

The difference in response is obviously a result of many factors, not the least of which is the meaning that I attribute to the event. The sexual response is learned. This is why it is often said that the most powerful sex organ is the brain. The brain receives input from all the senses and combines it with previous learning. The problem, of course, is for the brain to formulate a sexual response that is culturally appropriate without being sexually inhibiting. In any culture, a great deal of learning is required in order to bring about a balance between these factors. The point, though, is that our senses provide us with information that we interpret as being sexual. Again, nothing makes us automatically respond sexually.

Expanding Your Erogenous Zones

The knowledge that it is we who decide what is sexual can help us experience more sexual pleasure in our relationship. Let me explain why. Most of the so-called sex manuals of the past dealt with erogenous zones—the areas of the body from which sexual pleasure can be obtained when they are stimulated. These books usually located the erogenous zones in the breasts and the genitals. These, at any rate, are the places on the body that most people—particularly men—identify as being sexual. These are the areas covered up on the beach, or heavily emphasized in magazines such as *Playboy, Penthouse,* and *Playgirl.*

Emphasis on these areas of the body begins very early in our developmental process, usually in elementary school. The slang words used to describe these areas become part of most teenagers' vocabulary. The mere mention of such "private" or "secret" parts becomes wrapped in mystery, excitement, and fear. As children, we believe that these words and the parts they describe are taboo, and we begin attributing all kinds of power to them. So it is no wonder that by the time we are adults we consider the breasts and genitals the primary areas to be focused on during sexual activity.

Perhaps if women in our culture always wore ear muffs, the ears also might be viewed as sexual. How about the hands as an erogenous zone? They have plenty of nerve endings. In fact, when I was a teenager and the Beatles sang, "I Want to Hold Your Hand," the hands did become an erogenous zone for me. In some cultures, women do not customarily cover their breasts. This used to be the case in Polynesia, and is still so among many African tribes. In those cultures people do not immediately think of sex when they see an exposed breast.

Of course, the breasts and genitals are our primary erogenous zones. Few people will reach orgasm by having their faces or backs—or any other part of their bodies stimulated. But this does not mean that sexual feeling has to be limited to these areas. Remember there are no such things as sexual nerve endings; the nerve endings in the breasts and genitals are the same as the ones in the ears, feet, back, and stomach. Are the latter erogenous zones? They are, if stimulated in a sexual context, or if we define the stimulation we receive in these areas as sexual and pleasurable.

The entire body is potentially erogenous. We have nerve endings all over our bodies. Some areas have a greater concentration of nerve endings than others, but all can transmit sensation to the brain that can be perceived as pleasurable. Many people ignore this potential and instead focus all of their attention on sensations in their genitals. Holding the image of the body as one big erogenous zone can help us develop the ability to be sensuous. Many couples unfortunately lack this ability. The point of this book is to expand the range of sexual pleasure; one way to achieve this is to see the whole body as erogenous.

The Body's Senses as Sources of Sexual Arousal—Touch

We take in sexual information and stimulation through our senses. The first sense that we become aware of at birth is touch. The perception of touch is mediated through nerve endings in the skin and deeper tissues. How we respond to touching in adulthood is determined to a large degree by how much touching we received as infants.

Drs. Brant F. Steele and C. B. Pollock of the University of Colorado found evidence that inadequate communication with a baby through its skin is likely to result in inadequate later development of sexual functions. As Ashley Montague puts it in his book *Touching*, "The oft-heard complaint directed by women at the clumsiness, crassness, and incompetence of men in their sexual approaches and in sexual intercourse itself, men's lack of skill in foreplay and their failure to understand its meaning, almost certainly reflects [their sensual deprivation] in childhood." But of course there are other reasons for men's problems with touching, which we have already discussed.

One of the best antidotes for difficulty in touching in either the receiving or giving mode is to take a massage class. I did so in my early twenties, and it was a tremendous learning experience. I didn't become an expert masseur, but I learned how to touch in a sensual way, something I had trouble learning in the back seat of a car or in the living rooms of parents. Learning to touch in a sensual manner greatly improved my ability as a lover. It also helped me to better understand and experience what it means to be sensual in a sexual context.

Sensual Sights

What we see also plays a role in our sexual response. Visual cues can turn us on or off, depending on our preconceptions, expectations, and other factors. Men as well as women—and particularly those wanting to attract a mate—put a great deal of effort into their appearance.

Often, in my practice, I hear single women complain about what they call being in a "meat market" when they are in public places. They feel that males look at them as if merely to assess their bodies. Of course, men do like to look at women who are physically attractive. But, as I mentioned in chapter six, women respond to visual stimuli just as men do.

Therefore I tell these women to turn the situation around and stare back at the men who are looking at them. Put them in the meat market and check out their bodies from head to toe. Let them see that their physical appearance is important to you. I know it's not everything, but neither is it irrelevant.

In reality, the whole world is a meat market. Everywhere you go men and women are responding to visual stimulation of the opposite sex. What they choose to do with this stimulation is another issue.

Sensual Smells

The third sense from which we receive stimulation is the sense of smell. In the animal kingdom, smell often serves as a trigger for sexual arousal. Some experts say that there is no evidence that particular smells have any direct sexual affect on humans, while other researchers speculate that certain odors do play a role in human sexual arousal. These odors are created by pheromones, which are biochemicals secreted from the bodies of animals, and possibly humans, to create sexual attraction. The smell of pheromones need not be consciously perceived in order to have an effect.

Clearly, the general public believes that smells have an impact on sexual interest, since people of both sexes spend millions of dollars annually on perfume and cologne. I personally doubt that these artificial odors affect sexual arousal, except through learned response. Perhaps a mental association is unconsciously formed between a particular scent and a pleasant sexual encounter with a certain person. Of course, if the experience was negative, then the fragrance may have a sexually inhibiting effect.

If humans, like animals, have natural pheromones that influence sexual behavior, then their effect is largely negated by the things we do to cover up or remove our natural body odors. I am not advocating the deliberate cultivation of body odor as a way of heightening one's sexual attractiveness, because in our culture strong body odors can be offensive and can inhibit sexual desire. But perhaps you may wish to experiment with your sense of smell to better understand your reactions to different kinds and degrees of body odors, so that you can find your own natural balance between hyperclean and its opposite.

Sensual Sounds

The last sense that contributes to sexual stimulation is hearing. We humans do not use mating calls per se, as many animals do. Nevertheless, sound can have an erotic effect on us.

One study found that erotic audio tapes of explicit sex were effective in inducing sexual arousal in both women and men—more so than tapes containing merely romantic material. The experimenters' prior assumption that women would react only to the romantic tapes—or that they would prefer eroticism tempered with romance to straight-out sex—proved wrong.

I often hear how "sweet nothings" whispered in a lover's ear can be a real turn-on, particularly for women. For men, it is often their partner's moans during orgasm that really excites them. Certain types of music can have an arousing effect on some people, since, as we have already seen, what people do during or before a sexual experience can affect their sexual behavior.

Which Sense Is Dominant for You?

Over two decades ago, linguists Bandler and Grinder proposed that people process or perceive their world through one sense more than the others. They believed that in order to better communicate with an individual it is important to know which is his or her dominant sense. Once this is understood, then certain predicate words can be used in conversation to establish an atmosphere of trust and understanding with that person. This is one of the basic principles of what has come to be known as neuro-linguistic programming.

For example, if I were counseling a man who is predominantly a visual person, I would ask him questions such as, "How does your marriage look to you?" or, "Do you see yourself leaving the relationship at some point?" The key words in these two questions are "look" and "see"—i.e., visual references. The use of these words would create a sense of empathy between us, because they would show that I understand or share his visual orientation. For him, the effect would be entirely subliminal.

If I were to ask the same person how it "feels" or how it "sounds" to leave the relationship, he might have a much more difficult time answering the questions, since he would be unable to relate as easily to the senses evoked by these words.

All of this is relevant to what happens in a sexual relationship. Perhaps the best way to explain how and why is to use my own experience as an example. I tend to be a touch/feel type of person, so when I am sexually involved I tend not to verbalize what I am experiencing, though I may be enjoying the experience intensely.

My wife, on the other hand, tends to be more of an auditory or aural person; she responds to what she hears while having sex. In the past, when we were making love, she might be touching and pleasuring me, and I would be loving the stimulation she was giving me, but I wouldn't verbalize my pleasure. My wife, meanwhile, would be wondering if I was alive, let alone having a good time. She was unable to enjoy the experience because she wasn't hearing anything from me until after the fact, and that was too late.

When I realized what was happening between us, I was able to correct the situation by translating my experience into a mode that was accessible for her. I verbalized what I was feeling while we were making love.

Hearing what I was experiencing had a positive effect on my wife's sexual response. It wasn't necessary for me to carry on a conversation; that would be disruptive for both of us. But by verbalizing some of what I was experiencing I was able to build a stronger bridge of understanding between us. This enhanced my sexual experience as well.

Some Physiological Fallacies About Sex

Many people believe that men respond more rapidly to sexual stimulation and are therefore capable of reaching orgasm faster than women. There is no known physiological basis for this claimed difference, and in fact, females can respond as quickly as men do to effective sexual stimulation. If there is a difference, it may be that women are slower to admit that they are aroused. But even if it were true that women are slower to arouse, who wants to be in such a hurry in the first place, and why should there be a race?

Another fallacy I sometimes encounter is that the best type of orgasm is one that is experienced simultaneously by a couple. Physiologically there is no reason why this should be more pleasurable. Subjectively or psychologically, mutual orgasm may indeed be highly pleasurable for the individuals involved. My concern is that the couple don't make mutual orgasm their goal, because to do so tends to create rigidity in their sexual relationship. They become so concerned about their goal that they miss the fun and pleasure along the way. If simultaneous or mutual orgasm occurs, that's great, but don't try to force the experience.

Some clients have told me they believe that without mutual orgasms conception can't occur. Needless to say, nothing could be further from the truth.

One popular misconception is epitomized in a bumper sticker which reads: "Divers do it deeper." The idea is that the deeper a male is able to stimulate a woman in her vagina, the greater her pleasure. On a physiological level this belief has no basis.

The fact is that there are fewer nerve endings deep in the vagina than there are near the entrance. This makes biological sense: childbirth is already painful, but if the vagina were well endowed with nerve endings it would make it even more painful. Perhaps having a man's penis deep inside is psychologically pleasurable for a woman, but there is no physiological reason for it to be so. I see this common fallacy as an example of men's preoccupation with intercourse as the main form of sexual stimulation for women.

Freud's Fallacy

Sigmund Freud can be credited with one of the most widespread and insidious fallacies about sex. He made a distinction between vaginal orgasm and clitoral orgasm. Freud believed that during childhood girls experience orgasm by rubbing their clitoris, but that as they mature into adulthood their sexual stimulation should shift from the clitoris to the vagina via intercourse.

For many years, women who had been exposed to Freudian doctrine and who were experiencing clitoral orgasm during intercourse felt that there was something wrong with them psychologically because they weren't "coming" the right way. So off they went to their analysts to spend years trying to uncover the reason, usually with few results.

In a review of this unfortunate episode in the history of psychology Philip Slater writes, "Before Masters and Johnson undermined the dogma of the vaginal orgasm, two generations of women had felt guilty and inadequate because of a man's fantasy about how their bodies should function."

Masters and Johnson showed that the distinction between the two types of orgasms for women was physiologically nonexistent. All female orgasms are physiologically the same, regardless of the source or location of stimulation; there is only one kind of orgasm. Moreover, they found that clitoral stimulation is almost always involved in producing an orgasm; that is, the clitoris initiates the orgasm, although it may be experienced as well in other areas of the woman's genitals.

Since Masters and Johnson's original research findings, an area located on the anterior wall of the vagina, known as the Grafenberg spot (or G-spot), has been shown in certain studies to be highly sensitive to erotic stimulation, and to play a role in orgasm for some women. These findings are still controversial among sex researchers.

My position is that a woman needs to trust her own body's sexual experience. If she thinks she has a G-spot, then she probably does, and exploring it may offer her yet another way to enhance her sexual response potential. But I wouldn't want the finding and stimulation of the G-spot to become simply another goal. From a physiological point of view, intercourse is a rather indirect way to stimulate the clitoris, compared to manual or oral clitoral stimulation. It should not be surprising, therefore, that a large percentage of women are not able to experience orgasm through intercourse alone.

Women still seek the help of therapists because they aren't experiencing orgasms during intercourse. They have been made to feel that there is something wrong with them—and it is usually their sexual partner who has planted the idea. Perhaps the man feels inadequate as a lover because his partner doesn't climax when they have intercourse. I often ask such woman, "Have you ever had an orgasm before?" She says, "Sure I have, when my husband orally stimulates me, or when he uses his fingers and rubs my clitoris." Then I ask, "What's the matter with that?" "My husband wants me to come when he is inside me. He thinks he shouldn't have to use his hands or mouth."

In such cases I believe it is the man who is in need of counseling. He is operating under the false belief that he is adequate only if his wife experiences orgasm through intercourse. The idea that I would want to impart to both men and woman is that whatever way a person experiences an orgasm is fine; there is no correct or right way. Whatever works—and who's to judge? Only you.

Men's Common Sexual Problems—
Symptoms and Solutions

My purpose in this and the next chapter is to familiarize you with common sexual problems that we all may encounter in our lives. I also want to provide some understanding of the causes of these dysfunctions and some of the ways they can be treated. Since it is difficult to treat our own sexual problems without the help of a trained professional, I don't intend this information to be employed in self-treatment. Rather, my purpose is to help readers recognize certain dysfunctions and know there are successful treatments available.

Many sexual dysfunctions, particularly those of males, could be prevented if men had a better understanding of their own sexuality. As Bernie Zilbergeld states in his book, *Male Sexuality*, "The models of sex and masculinity that were and are presented to us are deficient in a great many ways, harmful to both us and our partners, and the main cause of our sexual dissatisfaction and problems. These models have little to do with what is possible or satisfying for human beings." I would like to add that the same things are true for most women.

Sexual dysfunction is a very broad subject, not one that could be completely covered in a book of this kind. For this reason, I have chosen to explore only the more common issues. Sex therapists and others wishing to have more extensive clinical information will, I'm afraid, have to go elsewhere for that. My purpose here is to provide a survey of common dysfunctions and their available treatments, not to offer a comprehensive clinical picture.

The Evolution of the Treatment of Sexual Dysfunctions

In the past, many professionals viewed all sexual dysfunctions as symptomatic of deep-seated psychological problems. The treatment of these problems required intensive, long-term psychotherapy that delved back into a patient's childhood to uncover the roots of the problem. The results of this process were questionable at best.

When Masters and Johnson came on the scene, the treatment of sexual dysfunctions was radically altered. These clinicians advocated treatment programs that dealt with the patient's sexual life in the present. They often focused on changing the patient's sexual behavior by prescribing exercises for the couple to do outside the therapist's office. This was a short-term approach with immediate results. Much of what we'll be describing in this chapter is drawn from Masters and Johnson's approach.

Like many other therapists, I have taken the therapy program developed by Masters and Johnson and adapted it to my own style. But when this immediate approach doesn't get results, I proceed with the more conventional approaches of long-term deep psychotherapy. You will find, however, that I have limited most of our discussion here to short-term therapy which in most cases is what readers will encounter.

Premature Ejaculation

The term "premature ejaculation" implies that we know the right time for an ejaculation to occur. But when is ejaculation premature? Is it premature if it occurs before the man enters his partner's vagina? Ten seconds after he enters? Two minutes? Ten minutes? An hour? Of course, any answer would be arbitrary.

Masters and Johnson define premature ejaculation (also called P.E.) as the inability to delay ejaculation long enough for the woman to have an orgasm at least fifty percent of the time. According to their definition, the man's prematurity is connected to his partner's opportunity or ability to experience orgasm. But what if she isn't orgasmic through intercourse? The man could last for an hour and he still would be considered premature.

Helen Singer Kaplan defines premature ejaculation as the absence of voluntary control. That is, the man has little or no control over when he ejaculates.

My concept of premature ejaculation is similar to Dr. Kaplan's. I, too, define it as the man's inability to control his ejaculation. The issue is one of self-control rather than time.

Common Causes

As with most of the sexual dysfunctions, P.E. can appear as either a chronic or an acute problem. When premature ejaculation has been a long-term problem, its roots nearly always go back to the man's early sexual development. Having listened to the sexual histories of hundreds of males with premature ejaculation problems, I have noticed a common pattern.

A man's first ejaculations usually occur through masturbation. For the man who has P.E., these early experiences were filled with guilt and anxiety. Therefore he was usually in a hurry, trying to get it over as quickly as possible so as not to get caught. He could never simply relax and enjoy for as long as he wanted to pleasure himself.

When he first experienced intercourse, the same conditions existed. Perhaps he was having intercourse with a girl in the back seat of a car, or in his or her parents' living room. Again, the experience was pervaded by the constant fear of being caught. At the same time, since he didn't know much about what to do sexually, he felt nervous or anxious. And so he has come to associate fear and anxiety with sex, and premature ejaculation is his unconscious way of minimizing these disturbing emotions.

Now he's on his honeymoon with his new wife. Again he feels anxious. He wants this experience to be memorable, and therefore, he feels pressure to perform. He cannot relax. Both because of his lack of confidence based on his past sexual experiences, and because of the anxiety arising from the present situation, he ejaculates prematurely. Gradually his prematurity becomes a consistent problem with his new wife. He becomes frustrated and develops a sense of inadequacy as a lover, and tends to lose interest in sex altogether.

The pattern worsens the longer it continues. And this is true for nearly all sexual dysfunctions, whether male- or female-related. The problem almost never takes care of itself over time.

The Vicious Circle of Premature Ejaculation

Premature ejaculation, like the other sexual dysfunctions, is a vicious circle. The circle goes something like this: When he knows that he is going to be sexual with his partner, the man starts thinking about whether he will be able to last very long. This could, for example, be at lunchtime before the evening in question. When he begins thinking about the upcoming event and his "performance," his anxiety begins to build. During the afternoon he is able to repress his anxiety somewhat by concentrating on his job, but (as we have seen) repressed emotions don't simply go away. When he comes home from work and sees his partner, he thinks again about the sexual experience to come later that evening and feels more anxiety.

By the time he and his partner are in bed together, he has created a great deal of performance anxiety for himself. When he does begin to interact sexually, his thoughts are centered mainly around not ejaculating. Having accumulated during the day his anxiety is now heightened by the circumstance of the moment, making him extremely tense. Since he cannot relax and enjoy the pleasure of the moment, he ejaculates prematurely, which confirms his earlier fears, reinforcing his insecurity.

The person suffering P.E. becomes goal-oriented. His goal is to not ejaculate prematurely. But the more goal-oriented he becomes, the less he is able to focus on the pleasure of the moment, and so he creates more anxiety for himself. The more anxiety he feels, the more apt he is to ejaculate prematurely, which causes him to become even more goal-oriented, and so on.

Explanations for Premature Ejaculation

The traditional psychoanalytic explanation for premature ejaculation is that the man has repressed intense, but unconscious, sadistic feelings toward women. These feelings probably have their origin in his relationship with his mother. The unconscious purpose of ejaculating quickly is to defile and soil the woman and deprive her of her own pleasure. While this explanation may be true in some cases, it most definitely is not true for the majority of men.

Some therapists see premature ejaculation as an unconscious weapon in a couple's struggle for power or control. The woman wants her partner to postpone his ejaculation so that she can experience more pleasure. The man, as a way of getting back at her for something she has done outside the bedroom, rebels and ejaculates quickly. Again, this explanation may be accurate in some instances, but not in most. Whatever the general explanation for P.E. (and I tend to agree with Masters and Johnson, who ascribe it to stress during the male's initial sexual experiences), one thing is clear: it is rarely caused by a physical condition. It almost always has to do with the individual's thinking and subsequent emotions.

Unmet Conditions

Some men experience sexual dysfunctions such as premature ejaculation acutely only in certain situations with certain sexual partners. For them, it is likely that their conditions for functioning sexually are not being met. As Zilbergeld puts it in *Male Sexuality*, "A condition is anything at all that makes a difference to you sexually. It can involve your physical and emotional state, how you feel about your partner, what you think you can expect from her, the type of stimulation you want, the setting you are in, or anything else. A condition is anything that makes you more relaxed, more comfortable, more confident, more sexual, more open to your experience in a sexual situation."

In most cases of premature ejaculation associated with situations, the initial problem is that the man's conditions are not being met. Here are a few examples, showing the sorts of conditions that can be contributing factors.

John is 35 and has been married for ten years. During this time he has learned from experience that when his wife Sue does things that irritate him, it is better to repress his resentments. He has learned this because whenever he does try to communicate his anger she blows up and withdraws emotionally until he apologizes for upsetting her.

When they make up after one of these verbal transgressions, Sue always wants to make love. Wanting to please her, he consents even though he is still feeling resentful over their argument. When they have intercourse, John ejaculates quickly, which makes Sue even more upset with him. John in turn feels inadequate as a lover and as a man.

What are the conditions that are not being met for John? The most obvious one is that he requires an acceptable level of emotional comfort. How can John expect to be emotionally comfortable with someone toward whom he has a great deal of anger? It is very difficult to be sexually intimate with someone you are resenting at the same time.

This is exactly what John's penis is trying to tell him. If John's penis could talk, it would probably say something like, "You want me to go inside this woman you are angry with and give her pleasure? You've got to be kidding! You might be able to force me in there, but I'm going to get out as fast as I can."

A penis's behavior is often linked to its owner's true feelings. The key to correcting most problems is to learn what the message is so that it can be communicated in a better way. Too often a man knows what the message is, but tries to ignore it because it isn't flattering to his sexual self-image.

Another example is Steve, who is 32 and recently divorced from his first wife of twelve years. Not having had many sexual relationships prior to marriage, Steve was really looking forward to dating. Sex hadn't been very good or frequent in his marriage, but he had experienced no sexual problems.

After he had dated a while he had his first sexual opportunity since his divorce. Though he was excited about this opportunity, when the magic moment arrived he became extremely nervous and afraid that somehow he wouldn't be good enough. He wanted to impress his new lover with how proficient he was at lovemaking, but he didn't have any idea of the kinds of things she liked sexually.

As a consequence of his emotional state at the time, Steve ejaculated prematurely. He felt embarrassed and inadequate as a lover and wanted another chance to prove himself.

The next time he went out with his new woman friend he thought about how he wasn't going to ejaculate so quickly. In fact, he thought about it the whole day before going out with her. He thought that perhaps if he thought about his job while making love it might make him last longer so that he could satisfy his partner thoroughly. Again he felt anxious when they went to bed together. While they were making love he tried to think of work, but again he ejaculated very quickly. On the way home that night he was angry with himself and subsequently became depressed. He became so afraid of failing that he didn't ask the woman out again.

What sexual condition was not being met for Steve? One important requirement for a good, pleasurable sexual experience is the ability to relax. Obviously this is something that Steve was unable to do in either situation with his new lover. He was trying to live up to unrealistic expectations that he had imposed on himself. He was trying to be perfect—which will give anyone a load of anxiety, create tension, and the inability to relax

One important condition that Steve needs to have met, and one that is fairly universal, is the absence of judgment. In Steve's case, the judgment wasn't coming from his lover, but from himself. He was furious with himself for ejaculating quickly, which only made his condition worse. He needed to learn to accept that, given the conditions, his sexual performance made sense. Accepting what is happening doesn't mean liking it, but refusal to accept it only compounds the problem.

The last condition that wasn't being met for Steve was, again, emotional comfort. Many men who have just come out of long-term relationships and are finding themselves newly single, have problems like Steve's. In his marriage he had been aware of no real sexual difficulties; it was just that sexual activity was infrequent, especially toward the end. But once out in the singles world, it was as if the newly single male left an emotional cocoon that his wife represented to him. Even if husband and wife fought or were unhappy with each other, there was a certain comfort inherent in a long-term relationship. The problem is that Steve probably thinks, as do many men, that being emotionally comfortable isn't necessary for having a good sexual experience. For some men this may be true, but not for the majority. So Steve has put himself in a situation that conflicts with his unrealistic expectations and with his own particular sexual conditions. He has set himself up for more sexual difficulty.

The Fear of Intimacy

So far we've discussed the more immediate causes of premature ejaculation. As I have already mentioned, there are also many possible deep-seated causes of this problem. We cannot examine all of these, but I would like to mention one that seems to crop up frequently, the fear of intimacy.

This fear is usually unconscious, so that the individual isn't aware that it exists, or that it is getting in his way. I am often alerted to the presence of the fear of intimacy by a man's tendency to put a great deal of importance on the symbolic meaning of intercourse. Usually to him it represents psychological commitment. It is really rather like the old attitude of the 1950s which said that when you have intercourse it means that you love the woman and that you plan to marry her.

If the man fails to follow through on these expectations then he is a "bad person" for using his lover. The fear kicks in when he realizes he doesn't intend to marry the woman. At this point he has trouble consummating the relationship through intercourse.

Since the fear of intimacy and commitment is many times unconscious, it may conflict with his conscious intent, which is to have intercourse with his lover. As a result of this conflict, he ejaculates right at the onset of intercourse or soon after penetration has occurred. He may have no difficulty sexually before intercourse because there is no conflict, but once intercourse is imminent the conflict surfaces physically and the problems occur.

Treating Premature Ejaculation

While this book is not intended to be used for self-help treatment of sexual problems, the following can give readers an understanding of what can be done to help men overcome this dysfunction. Full treatment is most successfully undertaken with the help of a trained therapist. Be aware of this, so that you don't set yourself up for another failure and more frustration.

Premature ejaculation is a common dysfunction and relatively easy to correct. Before most men get to a therapist with this problem they have often tried a number of self-help remedies that have failed to correct the problem. The most popular self-help remedy is to think of anti-erotic subjects—things like work problems, sports, or the words of a song. The idea is to try to mentally distract oneself from the sexual experience, presumably to dull sexual reactions and thus deter ejaculation.

This attempted remedy brings up an important question. Why is this man making love? Is he just there for his partner? If she just wanted a penis without any brain or emotions attached she could masturbate. The man who tries to postpone ejaculation by thinking non-sexual thoughts probably feels responsible for his partner's sexuality. He is willing to turn himself into a machine just so that his partner can have an orgasm through intercourse. His partner may want to have an orgasm, but I doubt that she wants a machine for a lover.

This approach is also goal-oriented. The man is so focused on the goal of not ejaculating that he is deliberately not paying attention to the process. He is willing to do anything to reach his goal; pleasure is entirely secondary. Indeed, a man may go to the extreme of numbing his penis so he can reduce its sensitivity and therefore prolong intercourse. This approach can back-fire. The individual tries so hard not to have any sexual feelings that he is unable to respond. Now he has not only the problem of premature ejaculation, but he may also temporarily lose the ability to achieve an erection.

Gaining Control

Instead of trying not to have sexual feelings, I suggest an opposite tack to my patients. I suggest that the man indulge himself with sexual feelings and have confidence that he can relax in the situation, assuming that his basic sexual conditions are met. As contradictory as this may seem to the man who is suffering from P.E., this process works.

For the man who ejaculates prematurely, the most important thing to understand is the point of inevitability—the point at which ejaculation becomes inevitable. The goal of therapy is to help the premature ejaculator know when he is getting close to his point of inevitability so that he can reduce his level of sexual stimulation. Usually a male who suffers from premature ejaculation has no sense of when he is getting close to orgasm, and by the time he realizes this, it's too late.

It is this sense of having no control over the timing of his ejaculation that is at the heart of the problem. It is the sense of having no control that creates anxiety and the inability to relax. He is like an inexperienced snow skier. When a skier has little confidence in his ability to stop, he holds himself back, and the resulting rigidity causes him to lose control. In any case, he is unable to fully enjoy the experience, because he is too worried about how he will stop. The fear reactions that are intended to keep him in control actually cause him to lose it.

When a skier finally learns how to stop, and has confidence in this maneuver, he is able to abandon himself to the pull of gravity and enjoy the sensation of speed. This is exactly what the man needs to learn to control ejaculation. It is of utmost importance that he learn how to do this and that he gain confidence in his capacity to choose when he will ejaculate—rather than putting all his efforts into trying to prevent something from happening that is a complete mystery to him.

The kind of control we're talking about here doesn't mean avoiding the full experience of sexual pleasure in the moment. On the contrary. The first step of therapy is to have the man practice ejaculation control when masturbating. If he is in a relationship with a partner who is willing to participate in the program, I then prescribe an additional exercise—which is to exercising the same sense of control with his partner. I suggest that the partner manually or orally stimulate the client up to the point that he feels the point of inevitability. Then stimulation is stopped until the urge to ejaculate subsides. Then the same cycle is repeated.

It is important to understand that when the partner enters into the therapeutic process, there must be no intercourse until the male feels confident about his control of ejaculation with oral and/or manual stimulation. Otherwise, he is just setting himself up for frustration and a sense of failure.

It is also important to understand that if a premature ejaculator misses and goes past the point of inevitability, it is okay—he will get another chance. Remember my analogy with the skier. When a skier is learning to parallel stop, it takes him a number of attempts to get the hang of it before it becomes habitual and automatic.

Masters and Johnson developed what they called the "frenulum squeeze technique" for use with a partner in the treatment of premature ejaculation. With this method the partner is instructed to squeeze the man's penis in the frenulum area, which is just below the corona ridge, for about four seconds. This is a successful method, but I have found that most people get better results with the stop-start method.

Once the client has developed control of his ejaculation by himself through masturbation, and manual or oral stimulation with his partner, it is time to move to intercourse with his partner. The procedure is similar to the other therapeutic situations. While having intercourse, the man is instructed to enjoy as much pleasure as he wants, but when he is getting close to his point inevitability he should cease any form of stimulation, withdrawing if necessary, until his urge to ejaculate has subsided.

The position recommended is the female astride position. With his partner on top the man is able to relax and enjoy the stimulation he is receiving. This will also make it easier for him to communicate to his partner when he wants her to cease stimulation as he approaches ejaculation. This communication will already have been established during the previous steps.

The idea of stopping while having intercourse is difficult for some people to accept because of their beliefs. Many people believe that once you start, there is no stopping until the male ejaculates. For a premature ejaculator, this belief weighs very heavily. Once he starts having intercourse he sees no option but to follow through.

When I tell a client that it is acceptable to stop stimulation during intercourse, it is as though a weight has been lifted from his shoulders. It gives him a way out and a way to control the level of stimulation he is receiving. Having the option of controlling stimulation, his anxiety level drops and as a consequence he is more able to relax and sustain greater levels of sexual pleasure without having to ejaculate. The more he can relax, the longer he can last during intercourse.

Another sexual belief that causes performance anxiety for the premature ejaculator, or anyone else for that matter, is the idea that the only right or normal way that a woman can experience an orgasm is through penile stimulation while having intercourse. Obviously, this attitude puts a great deal of pressure on a man to be able to postpone his ejaculation. If he believes he has no option in satisfying his partner other than to use his penis, he will feel a great deal of anxiety—at least until he has considerable confidence in controlling his ejaculation.

Even if he does have confidence, limiting his options could produce a rather monotonous sexual experience for both partners, which in turn could cause the relationship to become boring.

Once the man has developed the confidence to control ejaculation, there is one final step. This is for the client to learn to control the level of his sexual arousal during intercourse by varying the type of stimulation he is receiving. He can, for example, vary the intensity of stimulation by controlling the frequency of thrusting in and out of the vagina. He can also control what areas of his penis

receive stimulation by varying the positions he uses during intercourse.

By developing this kind of sensitivity he can enjoy sexual
intercourse for as long as he wants without having to withdraw
entirely. If he gets carried away he can always withdraw; the point
is that withdrawal is now only one of several options available to
him for postponing ejaculation.

Erectile Insecurity (Impotence)

Impotence, as it is generally called, is probably the most frustrating and humiliating sexual dysfunction a man can experience.
The word "impotence" itself gives some clue as to the psychological impact this difficulty has on the person experiencing it.

Like frigidity, the word impotence has negative psychological
connotations that further aggravate the problem. To say that a man
is impotent is to suggest powerlessness, a label that carries over
into his feelings about his abilities in the rest of his life. It is for this
reason that I propose using the term "erectile insecurity," which is
a more accurate description of this dysfunction in any case.

Erectile insecurity can occur in either of two ways. One is acute
or situational erectile insecurity, in which the man who has had
past success in attaining and maintaining erections is suddenly
unable to do so. The second form of erectile insecurity is chronic, in
which the man has had a long history of inability to attain and
maintain erections.

The chronic type is more difficult to correct through therapy.
The physiological aspect of erection dysfunction is an impairment
of the erectile reflex. The vascular reflex mechanism fails to pump
a sufficient amount of blood into the body of the penis to fill and
render the penis erect. This impairment usually occurs at the point
when the male experiences a great deal of emotional anxiety about
his sexual performance. The reaction can happen any time during
the response cycle.

Common Causes of Erectile Insecurity

The psychological impact of erectile insecurity is, as I stated earlier, potentially tremendous. The degree of impact has a lot to do with how knowledgeable the man is about his own sexuality, and particularly of his conditions for being able to be sexually functional. In other words, the more knowledge he has, the better he will be able to accept and understand his problem. Only a few men who have come to me for help started out with this kind of knowledge and understanding.

When a man is unable to get or maintain an erection, he usually feels inadequate as a man, lover, or husband. He questions his own masculinity and self-esteem. So it is not much of an overstatement to say that, for a man, everything in the world is riding on the performance of his penis. As Zilbergeld states in *Male Sexuality*, "the erection is considered by almost all men as the star performer in the drama of sex, and we all know what happens to a show when the star performer doesn't make an appearance. The whole show is cancelled—or, to be a bit more accurate, the planned performance gives way to an impromptu tragedy, replete with wailing and self-blaming, usually ending with everyone feeling miserable."

When a man has problems maintaining an erection, he becomes extremely self-critical. The "critical parent" that I discussed in chapter one comes into play. His internal dialogue goes something like this: "What's the matter with you?! Why don't you work, damn it?! You're just over the hill! She is going to leave you if you don't get it up, you jerk!"

The consequence of this self attack is a confusing combination of resentment, feelings of inadequacy and anxiety, followed by depression and a sense of hopelessness. The part of the man that is afraid that he won't be able to sustain an erection is like a frightened child.

There is another part that is demanding and is worried about his pride and ego. This part doesn't allow for imperfection and mistakes. I liken this part to a very critical parent.

When a child is afraid to do something the last thing a parent should do is yell at him. All this does is traumatize the child even more. But this is exactly how the internal critical parent behaves for the man who is having erection difficulties. It yells at the part of him that is a frightened child. The critical parent may so intimidate the inner child that he doesn't want to be sexually involved at all for fear of failure and further punishment.

Depression, Testosterone, and Erectile Insecurity

One common symptom of a male's insecurity about his ability to achieve erections is a secondary depression. As a result of all his self-loathing, he develops a great deal of repressed anger. This in turn translates into psychological depression, whose physiological effects create a vicious circle, which works as follows:

The presence of testosterone in the bloodstream activates the brain to cause erotic desire and motivation. At the same time, testosterone provides the chemical environment necessary for sperm production, ejaculation, and erections. Of course, testosterone is not the sole determinant for these phenomena—psychological and social influences also play their parts—but it does have an important function to perform.

The man's psychological state influences his testosterone level, which fluctuates considerably in response to psychic and sexual stimulation. When a male is in a state of depression, defeat, humiliation, or in high anxiety situations, the secretion of testosterone drops off. As we have just seen, a man who is having difficulty with erections is likely to have precisely these feelings. His psychological state sets off a physiological reaction which reinforces the very problem that is making him depressed and anxious. The greater his reaction, the worse the problem becomes.

The Partner's Role

Erectile insecurity also has a psychological impact on the man's partner. Again, the degree of impact is related to his partner's level of sexual experience and to her confidence in her own sexuality. Many women will be sympathetic and will try to downplay the situation. Of course her message may fall upon deaf ears because the man is so absorbed in self-loathing.

If his partner is not confident in her own sexuality, his inability to maintain erections may threaten her. She will begin to feel responsible and start questioning herself. "Is this caused by the way I look? He doesn't think I'm sexy anymore. Maybe he is involved with somebody else."

Some women will try to rescue the man. They may see themselves as Florence Nightingale, committed to curing the man. They may try all sorts of techniques to arouse their partner to have an erection. His problem becomes her responsibility, and her ego gets involved along with his.

Like those who play rescuer/co-dependent in other personal relationships, the woman eventually tires of trying to fix the victim's problem; she becomes frustrated and angry over the lack of results. At first she is very motivated and reassuring, but as one effort after another fails she becomes agitated and critical of her partner. This criticism quickly drives him further into self-loathing.

Some women rescue their partners in a different way. Instead of taking a direct approach and taking responsibility for his problem, a woman might try to protect him from his problem by not confronting the situation at all. She might treat the man like a child who is too fragile to be able to deal with the real world. She withholds the consequences of the problem and thus prevents him from having to face the situation and seeking psychological help to resolve it.

This rescuing pattern seems to work for a while, in that there is no confrontation or conflict. On the surface the relationship seems stable. But meanwhile there is no sex for either partner. Over time, this unmet need creates a great deal of hurt and then anger in the woman. If sex is at all important to her, this resentment will build and she will eventually explode. When this happens, her male partner will probably react by feeling overwhelmed and defensive, and will retreat into a depressed shell.

The message in all this is that any form of rescuing behavior on the part of the partner is invariably nonproductive. No matter what a woman partner does or says, it is the man's problem and he has to take responsibility for finding the solution. He is going to feel a great amount of pressure no matter what she does, because of his own expectations of himself.

When I say it is his problem, I don't want to imply that the female partner is uneffected. It is just that her problem is a different one. Her problem is the lack of sexual frequency due to his avoidance of sexual activity. This is a problem that she can do something about. Getting angry with her partner does little to correct it. What she needs to do is to direct her anger at the situation she finds herself in. She can change her situation with or without her partner's help.

Her best option would be to immediately confront her partner with her feelings about their relationship. A good approach is to suggest that they get into some sort of therapy—preferably sex therapy—so that their problems can be remedied before they become worse. If he won't participate in any type of therapy, then she needs to explain the consequences to their relationship if the problem goes unresolved.

Seeking Help

When a man finally decides to do something about his erection problem, the first person he usually seeks out is the family physician or a urologist. This is because he believes that the difficulty must be due to some physiological malfunction; he doesn't want to consider the possibility that its source is emotional or psychological.

The doctor usually does a blood test to see if the man's testosterone level is normal. He may then give the patient a hormone injection to see if that makes a difference. Sometimes the placebo effect can improve the situation for a short time, because it gives the patient a sense of confidence. But this positive effect, if it occurs, is usually temporary.

Along with a blood test, the doctor is likely to advise the patient to learn to relax. This is good advice, but it is hard to follow unless the patient is given specific instructions, and unless the underlying reasons for the patient's anxiety are addressed. Otherwise, the physician is only dealing with the symptom, not the cause.

In the end, the best a physician can do, once purely physiological causes have been ruled out, is to refer the patient to a qualified sex therapist.

An important way to determine whether the source of the problem is physiological or psychological is to see if the patient is able to experience an erection at any time other than when he is making love with his partner. For instance, does he ever wake up with an erection? Is he able to experience an erection through masturbation? If the answer to either question is yes, then the problem is most likely psychological in nature.

In the great majority of cases, the cause is indeed psychological. But when erection difficulty is related to a physical cause, the common contributors are emotional stress, fatigue, undiagnosed diabetes, or a low blood level of testosterone. Too much alcohol consumption will often also affect erectile capabilities, and so will certain medications for high blood pressure. The last two contributors dilate the blood vessels, making it difficult for blood to trap in the penis and provide an erection.

Certain neurological diseases such as multiple sclerosis will impair a male's abilities. Lastly, certain spinal cord injuries will make it impossible for a male to achieve an erection.

Confronting the Psychological Causes of Erectile Insecurity

As with premature ejaculation, the psychological cause at the onset of erection difficulties is often that the man's conditions for sexual functioning are not being met. When his penis did not want to become erect it was in a sense saying something to its owner. Most likely it was saying that in some way it was not comfortable with the conditions of intimacy with his female partner.

The conditions required for adequate sexual functioning vary from person to person, but here are some common ones that I have dealt with in my work:

• As we saw in our discussion of premature ejaculation, a man must feel emotionally comfortable with the woman with whom he is involved sexually if he is to function properly.

• He may have built-up resentments that he hasn't communicated to his partner that make it difficult for him to become aroused enough to maintain an erection.

• The man often also needs to be able to trust the emotional commitment of his partner. This is a problem for many single men who are trying to be sexually involved with women who are also seeing other men.

• Often when a married man is having a sexual affair, he has difficulties with erections. I ask the question, "Are you emotionally comfortable in this relationship?" and he will answer, "Sure, she is great looking and we can talk about all kinds of things."

The rest of the dialogue will usually go something like this: "Yes, but are you emotionally comfortable?"

"What's that got to do with getting a 'hard on'? You should see what a great body she has! I just don't know what my problem is."

"How do you feel when you are with her and not with your wife?"

"Well, at first it's exciting to be with her, but after a while I start to feel guilty and become somewhat anxious about my wife finding out about this other relationship and kicking me out of the house."

So I persist in questioning, and finally the client starts to really express his emotions. On the surface things appear to be okay, but underneath he is feeling guilty and anxious. These feelings are getting in the way of his being able to function adequately sexually.

I tell men in this situation that they are responding normally to an uncomfortable sexual situation. Hearing this can be comforting to some men, because they feel so inadequate and abnormal. For others, it can be hard to hear because they think that they should be able to function adequately no matter what the conditions are emotionally.

We have already noted the misconception that many men hold to, which says that they should be able to have sex any time and any place. Having "conditions" is, well, for women. This may have been true when a man was 18 or 20 and his biological drives were going full-blast and overruling emotional conditions. But as he moves into his thirties, forties, and beyond his sexuality is influenced more and more by his emotional environment. The more a man fights this fact, the greater the odds that he will be setting himself up for sexual dysfunctions.

But the fact remains that when emotional conditions aren't met, many men have difficulty with erections. As natural as this sounds, many men don't want to believe it. Then, when the causes of the problem aren't addressed and the erectile difficulties continue, other factors come into play, making matters worse. In chapter eleven I discuss these other factors in greater detail.

The Origin of Erectile Insecurity— A Typical Scenario

As with premature ejaculation, a self-perpetuating loop or vicious circle is created. The following is a scenario typical of many men who have come to me with erection difficulties.

Jack and Sue are in their early thirties and have been married for about eight years. They have a couple of small children and both parents work outside of the home. After working hard all week, they decide to get a baby-sitter and go out to a friend's house for a T.G.I.F. party.

As they are getting ready for the party, Jack is already feeling tired, but says, "What the hell, we hired the baby-sitter, maybe I'll get a second wind."

While at the party, Jack and Sue have a great time, since it has been a while since they have been out alone together. Sue is a little concerned about how much Jack is drinking, though. They dance together and enjoy themselves, but by midnight they have to leave to take the baby-sitter home.

By the time Jack gets back, Sue is waiting for him in bed with one of her sexy new negligees. She is feeling very amorous toward Jack after having had such a good time together. Meanwhile, Jack is tired from the long day, plus the dancing, and is feeling the effects of several drinks. He knows that Sue wants to make love, but he is not feeling very energetic. He also knows that Sue doesn't initiate sexual activity very often, and he hates to turn her down. Also, he has always believed that he should always be ready to "get it on," regardless of when or where.

Jack and Sue get into bed and start having fun sexually. But when they start to have intercourse, Jack loses his erection and he and Sue stop being sexual with each other.

Sue says, "Don't worry about it Jack. It's no big deal. You're just tired and probably had too much to drink. Let's just go to sleep." Jack feels embarrassed and sexually inadequate because this is the first time this has ever happened. He just wants to hide in a shell, so he rolls over and simply says, "Good night."

The next day, the events of Friday night keep plaguing him. He can't wait for Saturday night to come because he wants to redeem himself and his sexual ego. When it is finally time to go to bed that night, he has been thinking about this moment all day.

When he gets in bed he immediately starts pursuing Sue sexually. But while he is touching, kissing, and caressing her, his mind is focused not on the pleasure that he is receiving in the moment while he is touching her. Instead, he is paying attention to his penis—watching it, waiting for it to become erect so that he can have intercourse with Sue and make up for the sense of failure and inadequacy as a lover he still feels from the night before. It is as if his penis is on a stage and he has a big spotlight on it.

Jack's level of anxiety is enormous at this point. He has been thinking about getting an erection all day, and by the time he gets to the point of intercourse his penis is under such an intense psychological spotlight that it simply shrinks off stage with stage fright. Jack is surprised and disappointed. He doesn't know what is wrong.

As time goes on, Jack keeps trying and trying to get an erection or to maintain one, to the point where he just can't take the humiliation and sense of inadequacy. He begins to avoid sex with Sue, making up excuses or claiming fatigue when they both know what the real reason is. Neither of them knows what to do about the situation. hey hope that with time the problem will go away, but it doesn't.

The pattern I have just described is a common one. It can be avoided and corrected by the man simply gaining a more realistic understanding of his own sexuality. If his expectations of his penis were more in line with reality and less with the fantasy model of male sexuality this culture perpetuates, the problem would be avoided, or could be easily solved.

The erectile dysfunction pattern presented is another form of the classic goal-orientation loop described in our discussion of premature ejaculation. This time the goal is to achieve and maintain an erection. The more Jack works at trying to achieve his goal, the more anxiety he creates for himself. The more anxiety he experiences, the less pleasure he enjoys, and without the pleasure he isn't able to obtain an erection. The goal-oriented approach keeps him from enjoying lovemaking because he is focused on his erection problem, rather than the pleasure of the moment. He is like a driver trying to free his car from a sand-trap. The more the wheels spin to get out, the deeper the car sinks into the sand.

Treating Erectile Insecurity

When a man with erection difficulties comes to me for treatment, I first try to determine if has a chronic or an acute situational dysfunction. In the majority of instances, it is a recent problem, and thus the latter.

The next step is to determine the psychological environment in which the problem first occurred. I begin with questions like, "How did you feel emotionally with the woman you were with? Were you anxious or angry? Did you trust her?" If he is married, I try to get an idea of how he feels about his marriage in general. I am trying to discover what emotional conditions for adequate sexual functioning were not being met for this particular client.

Often, when erection difficulties are the presenting problem, the real problem is a relationship issue. Consider the example of Frank and Mary.

Frank and Mary don't spend much time communicating intimately. When they do, they end up yelling at each other and then not speaking to each other for days afterward.

Because they aren't emotionally close, Frank wants to make love to his wife to bridge the gap. When they do engage sexually, usually Mary just goes through the motions with very little feeling. When Frank becomes aware of Mary's attitude while they are making love, he loses his erection and becomes upset with himself. He then decides that he needs to go to see a sex therapist for his problem.

In the case of a couple like Mary and Frank, therapy centers on the relationship between the two, rather than just on Frank. It is imperative that their relationship outside the bedroom be intimate enough for there to be an atmosphere in which they are relaxed and comfortable emotionally during sexual involvement.

Marriage counseling often helps couples like Frank and Mary to open up their verbal communication on an emotional level. Only then do I work with the sexual problem.

In the case of a man who isn't in a monogamous relationship, we need to discover what his conditions for adequate sexual functioning are. Once these conditions have been defined, then it is a matter of pinpointing the specific ones that aren't being met.

The next step is to see if the situation he is in can be changed and, if not, to help him understand why he is unable to function sexually given the circumstances. The process is similar to that in a marital situation, except that few single men have partners willing to participate in a therapeutic program.

Breaking the Vicious Circle

Once the conditions for adequate sexual functioning have been met, the next therapeutic task is to break the goal-oriented loop. In therapy, when working with a couple, the first thing to do is to make sexual intercourse off limits.

Some patients react to this directive with a sigh of relief, because it removes the pressure to perform and to get an erection. Within the context of sex therapy, the client is able to let go of working at trying to achieve an erection, because he is given instructions not to get one.

Once free of the goal of achieving and maintaining an erection, the man can simply focus on the pleasure of touching his partner. Guess what tends to happen then? He gets an erection.

Usually, once he gets his first erection, he immediately wants to have intercourse with his partner, and to hell with what the therapist said! He acts as if he may never have another erection again. But in his hurried, pressured attempt to achieve his goal of intercourse, he stops experiencing the pleasure of the moment and becomes focused on penetration. He loses his erection, and again becomes angry and frustrated with himself.

Usually, when this experience is reported back to me in therapy, the patient is ashamed and embarrassed for not "following the doctor's orders." I tell him that it is great that he got an erection, but that I want him to realize what happens when he starts trying to force his sexual experience. I tell him that he can get lots of erections but that doesn't mean he has to do anything with them.

Erections normally rise and subside while one is being involved sexually. As a man becomes more mature, he becomes more subject to distractions that might temporarily cause him to lose his erection. As Michael Castleman states in his book, *Sexual Solutions*, "The trick to raising a fallen erection is to relax and ask for some stroking that arouses you. Lost erections tend to stay lost when men get upset, order them to happen again, or berate their lovers for not being sexy enough to keep them hard."

I want the client to feel so confident with getting an erection that in essence he can ignore it when he gets one—it is no big deal.

Some men who come to therapy because of erection difficulties respond differently when I tell them they are to have no intercourse for a while. Instead of being relieved, they get angry and defensive. They say things like, "I thought we were here for sex therapy! If we can't have sex, then what's the point?"

It is difficult for them to see that sex is more than intercourse. This is also an understandable reaction to having someone dictate the way they should behave sexually. The man in this case is having a hard time letting go of control and being vulnerable in the therapeutic process.

The awareness experience described in chapter five can be useful in breaking the goal-orientation process. This helps a client learn to keep his focus on the pleasure of the moment instead of thinking about whether or not he is getting an erection. This kind of thinking takes him out of the pleasure of the moment and causes him to lose his erection.

Once a client is able to experience erections confidently through means of stimulation other than intercourse, then it is time to include intercourse.

At this point I tell the client that it is normal for him to have erections that vary in intensity or hardness. This is because the sexual response cycle has various stages. If he happens to lose his erection during sexual arousal, it just means that his sexual arousal has dropped off; it is no big deal. He knows that he is able to get erections, because he has in the past. It is just a matter of focusing his attention on the pleasure of the moment, and on something that excites him sexually about his partner.

It is important that a man who has problems with erections remember that he has alternatives to stimulating his partner with his penis. The issues here are similar to those in the case of the premature ejaculator. Understanding that he has options in his ways of sexual stimulation results in a great decrease in psychological pressure about his ability to get an erection. This in turn enables him to relax if he happens to lose his erection while having intercourse.

If he wants to, he can then pleasure his partner using his hands or mouth, or she may want to start pleasuring him. In any case, the goal is not to get an erection. The focus is sexual pleasure. When the man's attention is directed toward sexual pleasure in general, he will probably get an erection, and if he so desires he may want to resume having intercourse.

To digress for a moment, I have encountered the belief that somehow a male should get an erection just by being with his partner, without any physical stimulation. This may be the case when the couple is first dating and there is a great deal of newness and novelty. Just the anticipation of a possible sexual encounter would be psychologically stimulating enough for a male to experience an erection.

This type of automatic erection is great when it happens, but to believe that an erection must or should always occur in this way is unrealistic. After a man has been involved with his partner for a period of time, he becomes fairly familiar with her body and her responses. I'm not suggesting that they aren't sexually attracted any more after the novelty and newness wear off, merely that there won't be the same kind of automatic erection, especially if there is a degree of fatigue.

As Michael Castleman states, "Many men believe that their penises should be able to rise to erection on command. In men's magazines and in pornography, men usually present their lovers with fully-formed, throbbing erections from the moment they remove their clothes." What the man who has formed his belief system from such fictions should remind himself is that he does not know what went on to stimulate that erection while the camera was off.

To summarize: The primary therapeutic strategy in treating erection difficulties is to break the vicious goal-oriented loop. Once this has been accomplished, the client will start to develop a greater confidence in his erection capacity. He will, through the treatment process, have a better intellectual understanding about his own sexuality, free of the misconceptions that set him up for sexual problems. If he loses his erection, panic won't set in, because of what he has learned. Instead he will refocus his attention on the moment and on experiencing the erotic pleasure he is receiving; an erection will naturally result.

All the preceding is based on the assumption that the man's more deep-seated psychological issues associated with his ability to experience an erection have been sufficiently resolved. Likewise, any relationship issues between the male and his partner must also have been worked through, so that a loving condition exists between them.

Retarded Ejaculation

The last male sexual dysfunction that I have encountered in my clinical experience is called "retarded ejaculation." This prob-

lem is fairly rare when compared to the other two previously discussed dysfunctions.

Masters and Johnson refer to this problem as "ejaculatory
incompetence." In this situation, the man has little difficulty
obtaining and maintaining an erection, and is responsive to erotic
stimulation. His problem is that he is unable to ejaculate, even
though he wants to have an orgasm.

Ejaculatory inhibition can appear in varying degrees. In its
mildest form, it occurs only in specific anxiety-provoking situations. In moderately severe cases, the individual's inhibition is
more consistent to a given situation and he is unsuccessful with
ejaculation during intercourse. The same person may be able to
ejaculate through oral or manual stimulation, however. In the
severest cases, the man is unable to ejaculate in the presence of his
partner and must masturbate alone in order to ejaculate at all.

Causes

Physiological factors rarely play a role in this dysfunction.
Usually the causes are psychological in nature. One such cause is
the fear of letting go or of becoming vulnerable to one's partner.
This fear may have its roots in childhood, when it manifested itself
as a fear of being abandoned by his primary love-object at the
time, his mother.

In adulthood, the unconscious or sometimes conscious fear
comes up again in the form of anxiety during sexual intercourse.
The man is already vulnerable, and to let go and ejaculate would
put him in an even more vulnerable condition. Fearing this, he
becomes anxious and is unable to let go sufficiently to enjoy an
orgasm.

Some men have difficulty ejaculating because they are so busy
trying to please their partner that they don't pay enough attention
to their own sexual needs. Their focus is on their partner's pleasure, not their own. They pay attention to their own pleasure just
enough to get an erection (which of course is essential in their

mind for giving their partner the "right" form of pleasure), and then they shift their focus to watching and monitoring their partner's reactions while having intercourse.

Once the partner has been sexually satisfied with as many orgasms as she needs, then she wants him to have an orgasm. The couple's mental focus now turns to producing an orgasm for him. Now he feels pressured to reach a climax. He becomes anxious and unable to experience much sexual pleasure and is therefore unable to ejaculate.

In some cases, retarded ejaculation is a symptom of a power struggle in the relationship. Consider, for example, the case of Joan and Bill. They had been married for seventeen years. Bill is a "very nice guy," as Joan would describe him. He has never gotten angry with her, at least not as far as she could tell. He has always done what she wanted, without much conflict. Their only problem is that when they have intercourse he rarely ejaculates. This has been a long-term problem, but it occurs more frequently now. At first Joan was sympathetic, but now she has become upset and regards the problem as a form of rejection.

In this example, Bill is expressing his resentments toward Joan by holding back. It is a passive-aggressive behavior that he probably is not conscious of and doesn't understand. He too wonders why his body won't cooperate and allow him to give his wife what she wants, as he does in all other aspects of their relationship.

Again we find the penis speaking the truth about how he feels emotionally. If Bill's penis could speak, it would probably say, "I'm not going to ejaculate into this woman and give her emotional satisfaction. I have so much resentment toward her because you won't express your anger about the things that bother you. Bill, you are so afraid of her. Well, I'm not, and I know that it really drives her nuts when I don't come in her during intercourse. Until you express your anger up front, I'm not going to ejaculate inside her."

Understand that this dialogue is occurring at an unconscious level inside Bill's mind; consciously he is probably unaware of this internal conflict.

Another example of an internal conflict is when a husband tells his wife that he wants to have a child but physically keeps experiencing the problem of retarded ejaculation. Again, his unconscious is using his penis as its mouthpiece. Unconsciously, this man doesn't want to have a child, for whatever reason. He may be afraid to let this fact come to the surface for fear of the impact it would have on his wife and their marriage, given the fact that she wants a child very badly.

This man is responding to an unconscious message that tells him not to ejaculate enough to impregnate his wife. As long as it's unconscious, he doesn't have to take responsibility for his action or to deal with the conflict because it's his body that is rebelling, not his conscious self.

Internal conflicts like these are the major cause of retarded ejaculation in my clinical experience.

Emotional Trauma and Retarded Ejaculation

The last common cause of retarded ejaculation I want to discuss is emotional trauma in conjunction with sexual experience. The trauma could have taken place either during the individual's childhood or in more recent times.

In one common form of childhood trauma, the man grows up in a very religious family that regarded sex as evil and dirty. The trauma itself occurred when this attitude was enforced during adolescence with constant watchdog behavior on the part of the parents as to what their son was doing sexually. When they discovered any kind of sexual activity, like masturbation while looking at a *Playboy* magazine or kissing a girl, they punished him severely—probably both physically and emotionally. For a young, developing adolescent who is very vulnerable about his sexuality, this type of experience can leave a major emotional scar that can last for a long time. In some ways, this scar is very much like the impact that rape, molest, or incest can have on a woman.

As a result of this childhood trauma, a man can have an internal psychological conflict about his sexual feelings. The adult part of him wants to be sexual with his wife, but when he becomes aroused, the little boy in his psychological make-up feels anxiety and guilt. This internal conflict manifests itself in the form of retarded ejaculation. He is able to get an erection, which is representative of the adult in him, but the anxious, guilt-ridden child within him causes him to have difficulty in ejaculating.

Emotional traumas that occur later in life can have a similar effect—as in the case of the man who catches his girlfriend or wife in bed with another man, or whose wife tells him that she is involved with another man. Often, the man in the latter situation wants to be sexually involved with his spouse as an attempt to hang on to her. He regards sex as a form of reassurance that his wife still loves him. The man in this case usually feels guilty about not being there for his wife both emotionally and sexually. Now that he is threatened by another man, he is trying to compensaste for his neglect.

When he is sexually involved with his partner under these circumstances the man may experience some form of sexual dysfunction, such as retarded ejaculation. Again we have an individual who has an internal psychological conflict related to his sexual feelings. One part of him wants to be sexually close because of his fears of abandonment, and he sees sex as a way of hanging on to his partner. Another part is afraid to let go and to become vulnerable because of his fear of getting hurt by his wife due to her lack of emotional commitment to their relationship. As a result of this conflict, the man may be able to get an erection, but is unable to ejaculate. The idea of relaxing and "letting go" creates too much anxiety and fear, which gets in the way sexually.

Treating Retarded Ejaculation

The treatment for retarded ejaculation usually occurs on two levels. The first level involves the resolution of the inner conflict that the retarded ejaculation represents. The key to this process is to help the client first realize that the inner conflict exists and to help him talk about the issues that he is struggling with. This realization process is extremely powerful and in some cases eliminates the sexual problem entirely.

At the same time as the client and I are working on this realization, we also attempt to break the vicious circle of goal-orientation. Usually the client creates a great deal of anxiety within himself, knowing that he will soon be involved in sexual intercourse and worrying about whether he will be able to ejaculate. By the time he is involved with intercourse, he is mentally so uptight that he is unable to let go, and therefore experiences retarded ejaculation. This again negatively reinforces his sexual experience so he loses his confidence and will be more anxious next time he is sexually involved. This pattern is played out over and over to the point where the individual wants to avoid sex entirely.

As with the other sexual dysfunctions, the way to break the goal-orientation loop therapeutically is to take the patient's goal away. This is done by setting limits on his sexual activity. This forces him to concentrate on the present, less on what lies down the road, thus abating his anxiety.

If the patient's dysfunction is related to some past emotional trauma, then the treatment follows a desensitization process where the client is taken psychologically back to the event that produced the trauma. The idea is to help the client express the emotions that he is still repressing related to the trauma. Once the situation is emotionally defused, then the present-day sexual event will no longer trigger unresolved feelings from the past traumatic experience, and the client will be free to experience and enjoy the events of the moment for what they are.

Women's Common Sexual Problems— Symptoms and Solutions

Preorgasmia

The term "preorgasmic" refers to the woman who has never experienced an orgasm, at least not consciously, through any form of stimulation. Masters and Johnson referred to this type of woman as nonorgasmic or inorgasmic. I prefer the term preorgasmic because it implies that the condition is temporary.

The majority of women who experience this difficulty lack a basic understanding of their own sexuality. This is usually because they never masturbated when they were younger, so they don't know what gives them genital pleasure.

Often a preorgasmic woman looks to a man to teach her, hoping that somehow he will be able to give her an orgasm. But of course, he doesn't automatically know how her body operates. Usually he will seek to provide her with stimulation with his penis during intercourse. But since intercourse is the least direct form of clitoral stimulation, it is usually unsuccessful in producing an orgasm in such cases.

No man will know exactly what will excite a woman sexually. Both partners need to know this. A woman who is preorgasmic needs to do her own sexual research. The best way for her to find out what gives her pleasure is through masturbation. Most studies done to date suggest that for women, masturbation is the most direct route to orgasm. It cuts out all the guessing.

In theory, this is a simple solution; in practice, there may be complications. For the husband to suggest that his wife "just masturbate for a while and everything will be fine," is bound to be met with some resistance. The woman's feelings about masturbation might have to be addressed first.

The most successful treatment I have found for preorgasmic women is for them to take part in women's group therapy. This type of program was developed by Lonnie Garfield Barbach. The group setting tends to break down the feelings of isolation and abnormality that women who are preorgasmic tend to experience. It also enables them to support each other through the difficulties of learning to masturbate, and of accepting the idea that it is healthy to give themselves pleasure.

When the preorgasmic woman's problem is beyond this type of treatment, she must look for deeper psychological causes. The following are some possible ones, but of course it is impossible to know the actual cause of preorgasmia without studying the woman's unique history.

In some cases, women feel inhibited about experiencing orgasm because it has acquired symbolic meaning. Perhaps she feels that she could only have an orgasm with someone she is in love with. Or orgasm may symbolize an emotional commitment that is frightening to her because it represents a threat to her sense of autonomy.

Sometimes the mere intensity of emotion experienced during orgasm is overwhelming to a woman. When she is close to having an orgasm, she shuts down unconsciously (or consciously) to avoid the experience. Her fear of losing control and of becoming vulnerable inhibit her.

In some cases, the experience of orgasm can bring up internal conflicts in the woman about her own erotic feelings. One such conflict is the madonna-whore syndrome. Psychologically speaking, part of the woman (the so-called whore) wants to respond sexually, while the madonna part of her is resistant. If the madonna aspect is stronger, then the woman is unable to allow herself to experience an orgasm.

Finally, a woman's hostility toward her mate may establish an involuntary overcontrol of her ability to experience an orgasm. As we saw in an earlier chapter, repressed resentments get in the way of experiencing full sexual potential.

All of these causes of inhibited orgasmic response require treatment in the context of formal individual psychotherapy. But in any case, whether the woman merely needs to learn what gives her enough pleasure for orgasm, or her preorgasmia comes from deeper psychological blocks, once she has successfully resolved her problem, she must learn to incorporate her newly-learned skills during interplay with her sexual partner. This is usually accomplished through general sex therapy approaches, which will be described later.

According to Masters and Johnson, only a small percentage of women's sexual dysfunctions are due to physical causes. The majority arise from psychological issues such as those previously discussed. However, two specific physical factors have been implicated as causes of female dysfunctions. One is the condition of clitoral adhesions, which block adequate stimulation to the clitoris. The other is inadequate pubococcygeal muscle strength and contractions.

In summary: Even though a woman has never experienced an orgasm, she may have a high sexual desire and fall in love, enjoy foreplay, and intercourse. A woman's experience can be conditioned easily and is vulnerable to inhibition. Usually she isn't consciously aware of this conditioning process. One of the primary contributors to preorgasmia is a woman's lack of knowledge about her own sexuality and her difficulty in taking responsibility for it.

Secondary Orgasmia

In this dysfunction, a woman has in the past had orgasms through various forms of sexual stimulation, but at present is unable to do so. Usually, this condition is the result of situational factors in her life. The following are some of those factors.

Causes—Relationship Problems

In most of the secondary orgasm problems I have worked with, the woman's inability to experience orgasm stems from the emotional atmosphere between her and her partner; it is simply not conducive to the expression of erotic feelings. Generally, the woman has been repressing a great deal of resentment and anger about her mate over a number of years. Gradually these resentments have built up to the point that she goes numb during any sexual experience with her partner. She may have had sexual feelings in the past, but no more.

Usually when she has tried to express her resentments, her partner has not listened in a way that made her feel acknowledged and heard. I discussed this situation in chapter three, where we considered the emotional groundwork necessary for good sex.

Lack of communication in one area of the relationship (in this case, her resentments) leads to an inability to communicate in other areas as well. The woman shuts off sexually because it is just too painful for her to experience any intense emotions with her partner.

In this kind of situation, I would seek to help the couple through relationship counseling before attempting sex therapy. My approach would be to help the woman express her resentments— both new and old—to her partner in a constructive way. At the same time, I would teach her partner to listen effectively so that she would be more inclined to trust that he will "be there" emotionally and not shut her out. Once she is able to trust that she can be emotionally vulnerable with her partner, she will be able to become physically vulnerable and let go enough to have an orgasm. The resentments are then not blocking her ability to experience pleasure.

Just as the buildup of resentment toward her partner can shut down a woman's orgasmic capacity, so can a loss of trust in her partner's commitment to their relationship. Such a loss of trust usually occurs after she has become aware of an extra-marital affair. Often, the wife becomes competitive and passive with her husband who has strayed. She tries to use sex as a way to hang on to him. But because of her loss of trust, she is unable to become vulnerable and to experience orgasm. She can be sexually involved with her husband, but can't let go, and then puts pressure on herself to be orgasmic. With this additional performance anxiety, she has created yet another barrier to orgasmic response. How long this condition exists for the woman depends on how long it takes for her to regain trust in her husband's emotional commitment to their relationship.

Obviously, this is not really a sexual problem, but a relationship issue in which the dysfunction has become the signal. From the client's point of view, the therapist should just "fix" her sexual problem; then all would be well. But unless the deeper relationship issues are addressed, the symptom will remain—perhaps disguised.

My approach to the problem would be directed toward restoring an atmosphere of trust between the couple. Once trust has been achieved, the woman's symptom of secondary non-orgasmia should disappear.

Another relationship problem that may inhibit a woman's ability to experience orgasm is a power struggle with her mate. We discussed power struggles in chapter seven.

A woman's perception of her lover may also impede her experience of orgasm. If she perceives her lover as stupid, untrustworthy, or crude, or if she is physically afraid of him, she may have difficulty responding to him sexually no matter how beautiful his body is, or how skillful he is as a lover.

Any of these relationship issues may come into play at any time in the course of a relationship and affect a woman's orgasmic capacity with a particular partner.

Vaginismus

The last dysfunction we'll discuss is vaginismus. This is a condition in which whenever the woman attempts to engage in sexual intercourse, the entrance to her vagina closes to the point that penile penetration becomes difficult, if not impossible. The muscles surrounding the vaginal entrance contract involuntarily; it is a reflex action and is not willed. In some cases, vaginismus occurs in connection with a related sexual problem known as "dyspareunia"—pain related to intercourse, experienced either during or after the act. Dyspareunia and vaginismus can occur either separately or together.

Vaginismus isn't a common sexual dysfunction, but when it occurs it is very disruptive to the individual's personal life. In the cases I have observed, the couple's marriage has been jeopardized because of the husband's frustration at the lack of sexual frequency resulting from the problem itself. This is not to say that a woman who experiences vaginismus is not sexually responsive; on the contrary. She may enjoy sexual activity and even be orgasmic, but the sexual experience doesn't involve sexual intercourse.

Sexual frequency tends to fall off because of the woman's feelings of sexual inadequacy, due in turn to her inability to have intercourse. Even though her partner may not complain, she still feels inadequate. There is an unspoken conflict not only between the couple, but also within the woman herself. Even though she enjoys sexual activity, she may avoid it because of her emotional discomfort. She finds herself in a psychological double-bind. On one hand, she wants to have intimate relations with her partner and is afraid that she will lose him if she doesn't; but at the same time, whenever they are sexually intimate she feels a great deal of discomfort and a renewed sense of inadequacy because of her difficulty with intercourse.

Sometimes a woman with vaginismus will seek therapy for the problem because the couple desires to have a child. A couple can avoid facing the vaginismus issue for years, but when the desire for children arises the issue has to be faced. Again, this places more pressure upon the woman to have intercourse, which only adds to her problem. The only way the desire for children contributes positively to the situation is that it forces the couple to seek help.

Treating Vaginismus

The treatment of vaginismus is usually carried out on two levels. One is a straightforward behavioristic approach of physical desensitization. The other approach, in process at the same time, is an emotional desensitization related to past traumatic experiences that caused the dysfunction.

The physical desensitization process involves inserting dilators into the patient's vagina. At first the woman is instructed to insert her own fingers—one finger at first, using lubrication. The idea is for her to be in complete control of every aspect of this process. She can insert her fingers as slowly as she wants, with no pressure. After she has become comfortable with using one finger, she may use two fingers, and then three, until she is thoroughly comfortable with inserting her own fingers into her vagina. This constitutes a major accomplishment for someone who has previously had difficulty inserting a tampon.

The next phase of treatment takes place in a sexual context with her partner. He is instructed to insert one of his fingers into her vagina, slowly. When she is comfortable with one finger, he adds another, and so on. The duration of this process tends to vary from case to case; it simply proceeds at whatever pace the patient is comfortable with. Once the woman is comfortable having her partner insert his fingers into her vagina and is not experiencing any pain, then she is ready for the next phase of treatment—intercourse. The couple is instructed to begin with digital insertion by the male partner. When the woman feels ready to have intercourse, the couple assume the female-astride position (i.e., the woman on top). This position gives the woman complete control over both the degree of insertion of her partner's penis as well as the amount and the tempo of thrusting. This sense of control is essential for a woman who is afraid of having intercourse because it has always been a painful experience. Once she is able to have intercourse pain-free, therapy is complete.

Specific Traps and How to Avoid Them

In this chapter we will consider some of the sexual problems we can all fall into if we are not aware of them. These are not necessarily deep-seated psychological problems, but they can be just as devastating if you are the one suffering them. If you do fall into one of these traps, the therapy prognosis is good if you seek the help of a qualified sex therapist.

Anxiety: The Emotion That Blocks Sexual Pleasure

We have already seen how the expression or repression of anger can affect a couple's relationship. Another emotion that can have an equal influence is anxiety. Anxiety and sexual pleasure are natural enemies. The more anxiety a person has, the less sexual pleasure that individual will experience. Anxiety can exist in mild degrees, but if not reduced or eliminated it has a tendency to feed on itself and intensify. When present, it can cripple an individual's sexual ability. Therefore, it is important to understand the sources of anxiety in the sexual context so that they can be eliminated.

188 • *More Than Just Sex*

The Fear of Failure

The fear of failing to meet one's own sexual expectations or those of one's partner is a common source of anxiety. This fear of failure has become more common among both men and women as a result of the sexual revolution of the 1960s; it is also partly due to Madison Avenue's relentless use of sex in advertising, and the increased alienation in our society, particularly among singles.

Sex has become the primary avenue for intimate communication among unmarried people. This adds tremendous psychological weight to an already sensitive aspect of people's lives by creating an expectation that each sexual encounter be incredibly fantastic. The problem is that about all it really produces is anxiety. When a couple get together sexually for the first time, they are moving into uncharted territory. Neither knows what the other likes or dislikes. They haven't built up a great deal of mutual trust, and this lack of trust inhibits their ability to be vulnerable with each other. They have made no commitment to each other, so each fears that if the sexual experience doesn't meet the other's expectations, the relationship will be terminated.

In short, in this situation there is an expectation for sex to be terrific, but there are also all the psychological conditions that inhibit great sex. It is no wonder that singles experience so much fear of failure. I commonly see this problem with newly divorced males who had been married a long time and had felt sexually confident in their marriage. Suddenly, they find themselves in the singles world among many assertive women—or, at least, that is how it seems to them. They have left the safety of the past marriage relationship and now have to worry about their sexual ability with somebody new.

Most men keep these concerns inside, which only adds to their anxiety. Their fear of failure becomes a self-fulfilling prophecy. They become so anxious that they are unable to get an erection, or they ejaculate prematurely. Once this occurs, they fall into the dysfunctional goal-oriented loop mentioned earlier, which may force them to stop dating entirely for fear of failure and embarrassment.

This same pattern of high expectation also affects women, but I have to say that I see it more often among men. This is probably because men more tend to feel that they are judged by their performance. This pattern can also happen to a couple on their honeymoon, if they have waited for this Big Night to finally have sexual intercourse. After a full day of anxiety and intense, exhausting emotions, there could hardly be a moment fraught with greater expectations and poorer conditions!

Dealing with the Fear of Failure

The remedy for this fear of failure may seem paradoxical. The person who is afraid of failure has to learn that failing is okay—in a way. Not that he should be thrilled by the idea, but he must learn not to make such a big deal of it. He has to be shown that the psychological conditions in which he is trying to function sexually are in fact setting him up for failure.

Sometimes it isn't just anti-erotic conditions outside us that cause failure so much as it's what is going on in our minds. An example of this is when a man who experiences the fear of sexual failure berates himself for being insecure. His internal critical parent says things like, "What's the matter with you?! Be a man and stop worrying!" This, of course, only creates more anxiety. To counteract this response, the man has only to learn how to be more gentle and patient with himself, overriding the critical parent with his own adult voice. This voice can tell him that because he is human he is going to have to pay more attention to how he feels in the sexual situation. If he feels uncomfortable, he should respect that and do what he can to correct it. Without that margin of emotional comfort, he's going to be anything but a sexual hero.

Another way out of the fear-of-failure syndrome is to talk about the fear before becoming involved in a sexual experience. For example, in the case of a man who is worried about getting an erection or ejaculating prematurely, it will help if he communicates his fears to his partner before they engage in sex. This enables him to stop trying to pretend, and to stop denying that he is anxious about failing. This may help him to relax. He acknowledges his fear rather than letting it run his life. If he has a loving partner who is accepting and supportive, this course of action will be particularly helpful.

In order to do all of this, the man has to be willing to become vulnerable and let go of his macho image. If he is not willing to do so, then he is simply digging his own grave, sexually speaking. To free himself from this fear of failure, he has to give up all his unrealistic sexual expectations. He is in the same bind as women who compare their bodies to those of Playboy bunnies and then feel inadequate.

Men who suffer from fear of failure have often formulated their expectation of how men should be sexually on the basis of the performance of a twenty-year-old. Given that expectation, who wouldn't feel insecure? They are not allowing themselves to be human; instead they are knocking themselves for not being the perfect sexual machine—which in reality doesn't exist. The fear of failure also relates to the issue of responsibility, which we explored in chapter four. As we noted there, it is impossible to be responsible for someone else's sexual experience.

Some men and women—though mostly men—feel that they should be perfect in terms of how they make love to their partner. But they don't really have any extraordinary knowledge or skill that would justify this belief, and so they have to guard against anyone, particularly their partner, discovering this truth. (Of course, their partner knows the truth anyway.)

So when the partner makes suggestions about ways to improve their lovemaking, the man takes it as a put-down and gets defensive. If this defensive posture succeeds in warding off the partner's suggestions, their own sexual ignorance remains intact. They have locked themselves into a tight sexual bind, resulting in fear of failure and anxiety. If left untreated, this bind can increase to a crippling level where sexual activity ceases altogether.

The way out of the bind is for the person to free him- or herself from the burden of feeling sexually responsible for the partner. This is done by realizing that the best kind of lover is one who is receptive to new information about pleasuring his or her partner more effectively. It isn't a fault or a sign of inadequacy if one doesn't know everything to begin with.

Demand for Performance

Another source of anxiety is the demand for sexual performance. A demand for sexual performance can come from one's partner or from oneself, and it can be imagined or real. Whatever the source, a real or imagined demand for sexual performance is crippling to one's erotic experience.

The physiological performance most men demand from themselves is an erection. The problem with this is that an erection is an automatic reflex; it cannot be produced on demand. Even though this is a simple physical reality, millions of men think that if they just keep pushing and trying, they will eventually get an erection. But they are often frustrated, because the more they demand an erection, the less likely they are to get one.

Again we find goal orientation getting in the way. The more demanding we are of ourselves sexually, the more anxiety we experience. The more anxiety we experience, the less sexual pleasure we have—and, for most men, the less likely we are to have or maintain an erection.

When this demand for performance is perceived by a man, whether from his partner or from his own mind, he will probably abstain from all sexual contact entirely. This lack of interest can be misunderstood and labeled as a lack of sex drive, but it is really an avoidance of an uncomfortable situation. This makes complete sense. Who would want to be in a situation where there is a demand for sexual performance?

Women also find themselves in a position where there is a demand for sexual performance. One thing that is often demanded of them is the sexual response of orgasm—usually during intercourse. Sometimes it is not only the woman's partner who expects her to have an orgasm through intercourse, but herself as well. She feels inadequate as a woman if she doesn't "come" through penile-vaginal stimulation. She may also feel that she has let her lover down if she cannot perform this way, since many men feel that if they can't bring their partner to orgasm through intercourse then they have failed.

Again, no one is responsible for a lover's sexual experience. Sometimes, because of anatomical differences, it is a physical impossibility for a woman to experience orgasm without additional stimulation—she just cannot get enough physical contact on the clitoral area to experience an orgasm. It doesn't matter how good her lover is in this case, because it's a matter of anatomy, not prowess.

An Excessive Need to Please the Partner

There is nothing wrong, of course, with trying to please one's partner, but when this effort becomes compulsive it can stifle the sexual experience of the overzealous pleasure provider. He or she can become so anxious about pleasing that it evolves into a sexual problem. People with this problem start worrying about their sexual performance because they don't want to disappoint their partners, either on the receiving or the giving end. And this excessive need to please the partner turns into a perceived demand for performance.

I have often seen men who have become so concerned about satisfying their partners with orgasms that their concern backfires on them. They continually ask their partners, "Did you come? Was it good? How many times?" As a result, the woman begins to feel anxious about having orgasms—"Is he keeping score?"—in order to please him, and her anxiety then inhibits her orgasmic ability. This turns rapidly into a vicious circle, and both partners become sexually frustrated.

Sometimes a person can become so concerned with the pleasure of his or her partner that sexual contact becomes a job, or hard work—which is hardly the point of sexual intercourse! This problem usually occurs for men whose sexual egos rest on their ability to please their partners. They turn themselves into sexual machines whose only purpose is to please. They ignore their own pleasure and then wonder why they are developing a certain amount of resentment toward their partners.

When one or both partners has an excessive need to please the other, the sexual focus becomes thought-oriented. Their thoughts are not genuinely erotic, but rather utilitarian, concerned only with the mechanical process of pleasing the other person.

These sorts of thoughts get in the way of the pleasure of the moment. Hence, the person becomes anxious and uptight, which defeats the initial intention. The partner can almost always read this tension, which inhibits that person's own pleasure as well.

For a man, this mental-sexual thinking might sound like this: "I can't come too fast; I've got to hold it a long time or she won't be pleased," or, "I've got to get an erection quickly or she'll think I'm not turned on by the way she looks."

The thoughts of a woman with an excessive need to please might sound something like this: "I have to hurry and have an orgasm or he will be disappointed with me," or, "I can't take this much time . . . he is getting impatient," or, "I can't ask him to go down on me; he will be repulsed."

Rescuing

An excessive need to please can quickly turn into rescuing. The person who has this need tends to view the partner as someone needing help, a victim who must be rescued from a pit of sexual frustration. The problem with being a rescuer is that you take on the responsibility of solving or fixing the problem of the victim. The rescuer then robs the victim of the chance to learn how to fix his or her own problems. Rescuing is another case of the attempt to be responsible for someone else's experience, and it tends to backfire. The rescuer tries and tries to fix his partner's sexual problem, and he gets more and more frustrated. This frustration can turn to resentment. Then a transformation takes place within the rescuer. He becomes a "prosecutor," being critical and judgmental of his lover for not improving. These are examples of prosecutor dialogue:

"I keep doing different kinds of things, like wearing sexy negligees, and he still isn't interested in making love. I'm sick of trying to turn him on!"

"I try this position and that position during intercourse and stimulate her clitoris with my hand until it is about ready to fall off, but nothing seems to give her an orgasm! I guess she is just a frigid woman!"

These are statements of people who started out with good intentions of trying to "help" their partners. They have a great deal of their own ego and self-esteem invested in their efforts. Their excessive need to please and to rescue is met with failure and frustration, and so they place the blame back on the partner they started out trying to please.

The antidote for the rescuing syndrome is to develop the mental attitude of caring enough not to care. On the surface this paradoxical statement sounds heartless, but it is just the opposite. For most people, caring means doing something for the person they care about. In some cases, helpful action does need to be taken; but often such action can create unforeseen problems. In the case of sexual rescuing this is nearly always the case. If your sexual partner is experiencing some type of sexual dysfunction, you have to care enough to let your partner fix his or her own problem, rather than taking responsibility for it yourself. By jumping in and taking that responsibility away from your partner, you rob your love of his or her own power to own up to the problem and seek lasting solutions.

Caring enough not to rescue the person you love frees you and your partner from performance anxiety and the demand for sexual goals. So often when someone cares too much, the partner having trouble feels a tremendous pressure to perform, to the degree that he or she may become inhibited and soon begin resisting any sexual involvement.

Spectatoring

If we're going to have a good sexual experience, we need to be able to let ourselves be vulnerable. We need to be free of all distracting thoughts and lose ourselves in the moment. Sometimes, however, we worry about our sexual ability or our attractiveness, remaining outside the experience mentally, monitoring our emotions and watching the other person's as well. This behavior is known as "spectatoring."

In spectatoring, one part of us is watching how we are responding sexually, another part is watching our partner, and still another part is watching how we are interacting. We may have an entire gallery of fragmentary selves watching the sexual event— with none of them actually participating.

The spectatoring person is in his head, barely making contact with his body. Naturally, his sexual feelings will become dulled. He is so busy watching and thinking that he forgets to experience. It should be no surprise that he may not be able to let go and respond fully. Often he will not be able to achieve or maintain an erection. Similarly, a spectatoring woman may have difficulty experiencing orgasm.

Spectators do not mentally stand outside of themselves for the purpose of sexual arousal, as in voyeurism. Instead, they tend to be sexually insecure, with a poor body image, or simply be the victims of perfectionism. When he is watching his own or his partner's sexual behavior, he is taking a judgmental stance. As a result, his freedom and ability to be vulnerable and uninhibited are highly limited, to say the least.

If the spectator's partner becomes aware of this process, he or she may also become inhibited and resistant to being involved sexually. Sometimes this will happen to a woman who feels that her body isn't perfect and knows that her husband tends to be a spectator or perfectionist. She may want the room to be dark when they make love. She resents his criticism, but represses the resentment. As a result, her sexual desire becomes blocked and she loses interest in being sexually involved with her husband, and possibly in sex altogether. When this occurs, her husband criticizes her even more, calling her frigid, which only compounds the problem.

Sometimes spectatoring serves as an escape. A person may use spectatoring as a defense mechanism in an uncomfortable situation. I find this to be the case with many women who have difficulty saying no to their partner's sexual advances. They give their bodies, but their minds are on something else—perhaps the shopping list. Why do they get involved in the first place? There may be many reasons, but the one I am given most often is that it is easier in the moment to give in than it is to refuse and then have to deal with the repercussions. This may seem a satisfactory solution on a short-term basis, but the long-term consequences are incredibly destructive both to the woman's sexuality and to the couple's relationship.

A man may use the same spectatoring technique, but for a different reason, when he is experiencing premature ejaculation. He tries to remove himself from the sexual experience mentally so that he can control the degree of stimulation he is receiving, and thereby postpone ejaculation.

The antidote for spectatoring is to find the issues that are causing the person to avoid fully participating. What are they avoiding through sexual spectatoring? What is the pay-off? Once these issues have been resolved, which will probably require psychotherapy, then they can refocus their attention. For those who become sexual spectators only occasionally, the awareness exercise described in chapter three may be useful.

Perfectionists who become spectators need to readjust their attitudes and expectations so that they are more in line with reality. They need to realize that there is no perfect body, and no perfect sexual experience. As Virginia Satir wrote in her book, *Peoplemaking*, "Whenever you look for perfection you always find imperfection."

Every sexual experience is unique and special unto itself. The perfectionist tends to set up one real or imagined sexual experience as the ideal against which all others are to be compared. Disappointment is thus inevitable.

Perfectionism is equally deadly when it relates to one's body image and self-esteem. So often I hear people complain that they are too small, too big, too skinny, or too fat. They are never satisfied with how their bodies look. They always point out some imperfection, whether it be a stretch mark here or a tiny scar there. As an associate of mine, Sheilah Fish, says, "They focus on the hole instead of the doughnut." They are missing the big picture. When we compare ourselves to models in advertisements, or in *Penthouse* and *Playboy* centerfolds, we are guaranteeing ourselves an experience of inadequacy. Sometimes it helps to remind the perfectionist that those photos in magazines are well-doctored by an airbrush artist before they go into print. Without that final touch the perfect body would never exist.

It is difficult—especially for younger people—to realize that there is no such thing as perfection when it comes to bodies. Our daily lives are so saturated, via television and magazine advertising, with images of the ideal male and female physique, that we lose touch with reality. Perhaps if more people belonged to nudist colonies they would get a better perspective.

The point is to enjoy what assets you have and accept yourself exactly the way you are. Tell that perfectionist spectator to get lost, because it is getting in the way of your enjoying yourself sexually.

Communication Breakdowns That Block Sexual Pleasure

Most couples find intimate verbal communication difficult. Talking specifically about sex is harder still. This despite the fact that discussions about sex on television have become increasingly candid. Afternoon talk shows describe the perfect orgasm and advise how to have great sex until you are a hundred years old. Unfortunately, the effect of this "tabloid" approach to sex is often that still more imaginary standards are created. The message that many of us get is that if we aren't having terrific sex all the time, then our relationship is in trouble, or we aren't part of a well-matched couple. Just as there are no perfect bodies, there is no perfect sexual relationship. When someone on television or in a magazine article or a book says there is no excuse for not having great sex, it makes it harder than ever for a couple to admit that they have a problem. It is easier for them to pretend that they are like everyone else—that is, like all the other people who are presumably having fantastic sex and who communicate well.

But when such a couple cannot talk intimately, they tend to make assumptions about what their partner wants sexually. Such assumptions create problems, because neither person ends up receiving or giving what they really want.

Such assumptions may be based on what was true in the beginning of their relationship, but without continuing intimate communication these assumptions have no way of being updated to fit both partners' changing attitudes and feelings. Since sexual preferences can change, it is important to regularly check out your assumptions about what your partner likes. Even long-standing couples can discover that they were incorrect in their outdated assumptions.

I ask virtually every person who comes into my office, "Are you able to ask your partner to give you pleasure in specific ways?" My goal is to determine the level of sexual communication present in the relationship. For the majority of couples in sex therapy, the answer to this question is no.

A couple's inability to communicate sets them up for routine, predictable sex. Their effectiveness at giving each other pleasure is greatly reduced. They tend to make love as if they are in a fog, automatically going through the same motions over and over with little thought about exactly what they are doing.

For people who are unable to communicate sexually, the thought of straying from the beaten track and asking for something different from their partner is extremely threatening. Often the partner who desires a certain kind of sexual contact is afraid that the other partner will think them selfish, demanding, or perhaps even perverse.

The way to break through this fear is to make it clear to your partner that just because you ask for something does not mean that you require compliance. You are simply offering information about what feels good to you, and your partner can use this information in whatever way feels comfortable. If you do go about your sexual communication with the attitude that you expect to get everything you ask for, then you are indeed being selfish and aggressive. If this is your expectation of sex, then it is probably best that you live alone!

On the other hand, not expressing your desires leaves your sexual experience a mystery to your partner. This will set him or her up for a sense of frustration and failure because then your partner doesn't know how to give you what you want. As we saw in chapter four, many women are afraid to express their sexual desires verbally because they don't want to hurt their partner's feelings. They are afraid that they will make him feel inadequate at his job of being the all-knowing sex expert. Another fear is that if these women express themselves verbally, they will be judged as being less feminine or will be considered "bad girls."

Sometimes a woman expresses her sexual desires verbally, but feels she was rejected. Asking for what you want puts you in a vulnerable situation, so it seems less stressful and safer simply not to be assertive. Many men also fall into this thinking. The problem with this non-assertive, self-protective approach is that it stunts the growth and activity in a sexual relationship. You may be protecting yourself from the emotional pain of rejection, but at the same time you are cheating yourself out of a fulfilling sexual life.

When your expressed desires have not been met, you need to ask yourself: Is this rejection, or merely disappointment? These are two entirely different outcomes in terms of emotional impact and consequences, yet which one you experience hinges largely on a momentary reaction based on prior assumptions.

You can set yourself up to feel rejected in situations in which you are not in fact being rejected at all. Most likely, your partner is not saying no to you as a lover; he or she is simply saying no to what you want. Remember, just because you ask for something, that doesn't require the other person to give it. But remember also that if you don't ask, you will seldom receive what you want and need—unless, of course, you happen to be sexually involved with a psychic.

Our fears of talking about sex tend to be strongest while we are in the midst of sexual interaction. To overcome these fears, it is important to understand the emotional costs in the long run if these fears are left unresolved. Take the example of the woman doesn't want to threaten her partner or make him feel inadequate as a lover. After a period of time of not getting her sexual needs fulfilled, she will probably lose interest in her partner. Her sexual apathy will then be taken very personally by her partner, since he will not understand the reasons for her lack of interest. By protecting him from the relatively minor discomfort that her communication of her needs might have provoked, she has set up a situation in which he will be far more deeply hurt in the long run because of her lack of sexual interest.

Many women have told me in therapy that they gave their partner specific verbal instructions as to what gives them sexual pleasure, but with poor results. A woman might say, "I told him to touch my clitoris gently, not as if he were polishing a car, but he keeps doing it the same way. What is the point of communicating? He just ignores me."

We can all understand this woman's frustration, but I would advise her to keep trying to communicate with him. She does need to stop participating sexually if her partner does not respect her desires, or does not tell her honestly when he doesn't want to do what she requests, or he ignores her.

Many men feel that they know the right way to stimulate their present partner, based on some successful experience with a previous lover. They have established a certain sexual procedure from this prior experience and apply it to subsequent lovers. It is as though they have made a sexual template. They may even pressure their new partner by putting her down with words like,"It worked for her, why not for you?"

What the man doesn't understand is that every individual is different in terms of what is sexually pleasurable. A certain kind of sexual stimulation will feel great one time but not the next. When a man thinks he knows the right way to pleasure a woman, based on his past experience and then his new partner tells him something that she would like that is not part of his usual procedure, he feels threatened and inadequate. He does not want to go outside of his comfortable realm of sexual experience. But this is exactly what she wants him to do. He may initially agree to do what she asks because he doesn't want to appear scared or threatened. But as soon as that specific interaction is concluded, he reverts back to his safe old sexual procedure, hoping that it will eventually be successful.

When it becomes obvious that he is unsuccessful at pleasuring his new partner, he feels even more inadequate. He has traded his fear of experimenting for the feeling of inadequacy. On top of all this, he has lost the trust of his partner, who feels he is incapable of listening to her needs and wants. This seems a heavy price to pay for being afraid and unwilling to be vulnerable to experimenting in the first place.

To summarize: It is essential, in establishing a long-term pleasurable relationship, to open yourself to communicate with your sexual partner. Frank, open talk is the vehicle by which we get the information necessary to give our lovers pleasure throughout the relationship. Because this information changes all the time, there needs to be a constant updating in order to stay current with our partner's changing desires and physical needs. It is the continual exchange of information that keeps a couple from falling into a predictable sexual routine.

I don't mean to suggest that you and your partner need to forcibly maintain a constant discussion of your sexual wants and desires. My point is just that direct and clear verbal communication is necessary, especially at the beginning of a relationship when you know so little about each other. But after a while, merely a few comments here and there may be all that is required—"Oh, that feels great!", or, "A little harder, please."

Small directional cues will usually suffice. If you become too verbally focused, then you will be thinking so much that you may forget to actually experience the physical pleasure of what you are doing. In addition, there are non-verbal ways of communicating. Good lovers can read the non-verbal cues of their partners in order to get information as to how their partner is experiencing certain physical stimulation. Non-verbal signals can include heart rate, breathing rate, muscular tension, facial expressions, and sounds such as moans and groans. Also, moving your partner's hands in a directive way can give indications about what you want.

If there is a single principle that holds true throughout this discussion, it is that where long-term relationships are concerned there's a good reason that sexual intercourse is described as "making love." Without caring and respect for ourself and our partner, there is little chance of enjoying any depth of sexual intimacy. That caring and respect require self-understanding, self-responsibility, and a genuine interest in our partner's, as well as our own, human needs, human weaknesses, and human strengths. When all this comes together in the playful, pleasure-oriented way that our sexuality offers, there are few activities more fulfilling.

Taking Your Passion
and Making It Happen

Thus far we have discussed many ideas about achieving fulfilling sexual relationships. To a large extent, we've explored them out of context, that is, as isolated events in a person's life. In this chapter we'll be taking a slightly different approach, showing how we might put them all together in a couple's therapy program. Rather than being intended for self-help, I offer this information for couples who want to enrich an already good sexual relationship, and for couples who are experiencing problems and want a mental picture of what would be involved if they sought the help of a qualified sex therapist.

The basic format of this material was taught to me by Drs. Tom and Thea Lowry, who worked with Masters and Johnson in the early '70s. I have altered certain parts to make the program more effective for my clients. Some therapists call the techniques of this program "sensate focus" exercises. I see them as more than that, helping people restructure their sexual relationships.

Most couples who come to me for help seem to have set routines in the way they make love. While these routines are not necessarily bad, their predictability hardly fosters excitement. When couples are experiencing real difficulties, the routines they have established are usually not just lackluster but actually anti-erotic, inhibiting sexual pleasure. For them, it is imperative that they restructure the ways in which they are sexually involved.

A couple can go about restructuring their sexual relationship in a step by step progression, moving on to the next step only when they have successfully completed the one they are on. Success occurs at the point at which they have both become comfortable and have had pleasure doing the prescribed exercises.

The couple should have no goals while going through the therapeutic process. While the therapist does have goals in mind, the couple's responsibility is simply to experience pleasure. People entering therapy tend to be very goal-oriented. They are so focused on their problem that this focus itself becomes an obstacle. They have worked and worked on their own to achieve improvement in their sexual relationship, but to no avail. By the time they seek therapy, they are very frustrated, and it is difficult for them to let go of their goals.

It is important for a couple experiencing difficulties to understand that no one is to blame for their problems. All blaming must cease. Both people in a relationship contribute to every aspect of that relationship, the good and the bad. It may be hard for each one to see his or her contribution to the problem but until blaming stops it is almost impossible to establish an atmosphere of emotional comfort and vulnerability. The absence of blame allows each person to make changes in his or her behavior without having past mistakes brought up again. As Dr. Tom Lowry used to say, "It took both of you to get off track, so it's going to take both of you to get back on."

Another prerequisite for participating in this process is that the couple be in relatively good emotional shape. A couple at war are not good candidates for sex therapy. If one of the partners has recently had an affair that the other partner has discovered, they are likewise poor candidates. These couples will probably get the best results if they seek out marriage counseling first. Two people have to be lovers outside the bedroom before they can be good lovers in the bedroom. Emotional well-being is the foundation from which sex therapy proceeds.

I will describe the process using an example couple, John and Jane, speaking as though they were in my office going through the therapy process. Assuming that John and Jane have met the above criteria and are good sex therapy candidates, we are ready to start the program. In the example that follows, it was determined through mutual consent that Jane would take the initiative and that she would take responsibility for details such as preparing the atmosphere in the bedroom. While it doesn't matter which partner starts, there will usually be one or the other who will volunteer. Very often, this turns out to be the person who sought help from the therapist and made the first appointment.

Step One

Jane, some time in the next few days I would like you to initiate the following exercise with John. And John, if you are not interested at the time Jane initiates it, than say no to her request. If you are neutral about participating, then lend yourself to the experience and see what happens. It is important that both of you want to participate.

Jane, I would like you to create a setting that is inviting for you and John to be sexual. Check the lighting. You don't want it to be too bright, so that you feel as if you are on an operating table, or too dark, so that you can't see your partner's body. In addition to the lighting, the temperature of the room is very important. It can't be too cold, because then it might not be comfortable to remove your clothes. Along with the lighting and temperature, Jane, you might also want to attend to things that promote a feeling of romance and sensuality, such as candles and soft background music, incense, or whatever works for you and John.

I want you to choose a time to be together when you won't be watching the clock. If you are thinking about the time, it will get in the way of enjoying the experience to its fullest. If you feel you are in a hurry, it might be best not to start this exercise until you have more time.

Privacy is another important factor. If you or John are worried that one of your children will walk in on you, you're going to feel inhibited and it will limit your level of pleasure. If you need to put a lock on the bedroom door for comfort, then do so. You need to feel that you have some place that belongs just to the two of you, as a couple.

Assuming all the necessary criteria have been met, Jane, you are ready to begin. You and John are in a nice, comfortable setting, with no particular place to go or be other than with each other.

I want both of you to be naked. Clothes only get in the way. In whatever position you both find comfortable, I want you, Jane, to touch John's body for your own pleasure and information. I don't want you to try to turn him on sexually or to give him an erection or an orgasm. I don't want you to think of him at all. I want you to pay attention to what you find pleasurable.

Now, when Jane is touching you for her own pleasure, John, I want you to agree to something. I want you to agree to communicate with Jane in a non-verbal way when you are finding her touch unpleasurable to you. Do this by gently moving her hand to another location on your body.

Jane, given that John has agreed to communicate to you if he is having a problem with your touching him, you can free yourself from worrying about John. If he leaves your hand alone, everything is fine with him. So, back to touching John. I want you to touch him all over his body, from head to toe if you like. The only exception is that I want you to stay away from his genitals. For now, that area is off limits. Everywhere else is great.

Touch his face, his back, and chest all the way down to his feet. If you are using your hands to touch him, make the nerve endings in your fingers act like amplifiers. I want you to notice what feels soft, smooth, warm, hairy, hard—notice every detail and nuance. Fully concentrate on what you feel—not on what you think or perceive in your environment.

(I often refer clients to the awareness experience described earlier in this book. Its application can be invaluable for this exercise.)

I recognize that having someone tell you how to touch your husband may seem awkward. I expect that when you first start touching John, you may not feel comfortable. I hope you are comfortable, but if you are not, I understand. I realize also that this experience may seem clinical, unromantic, programmed, not spontaneous or sporty, but that is okay. It is something new and different and a certain amount of discomfort and doubt is normal. I want you to go through the awkward stage until you start to relax, and then continue as long as you like, just touching John for your own pleasure. Jane, you can touch John as long as you want to and as long as it is comfortable for John. When you are ready to, you can stop. When Jane is done touching you, John, it is now your turn to touch her.

While touching refrain from talking. Use no verbal instructions or comments whatsoever. When people start verbalizing during a sexual experience, their mental focus tends to shift from what they are feeling to what they are thinking. This shift can inhibit them from fully experiencing the touching.

When Jane is touching John for her pleasure, or John is touching Jane, the person being touched should be aware of what he or she is feeling, open to the pleasure of this experience while following the instructions to gently move the toucher's hand to a different location if something is not pleasurable.

John, now that it is your turn to touch Jane, follow the same touch procedure that Jane did, but with a few exceptions. Again, you are touching her for your own pleasure. You are not trying to arouse her or give her an orgasm. You have no goals, only the experience of the pleasure of the moment.

Jane, if John is touching you in a place or in a way that is not pleasurable to you, then you will agree to move his hand to a more neutral place. So, John, since you do not have to be worrying about what you are doing to Jane, you can be uninhibited in your pleasure. You will not have distracting thoughts such as, "She is irritated with the way I touch her," or, "She hates it when I touch her stomach lightly." You can assume that if Jane does not move your hand away, you are not doing anything that bothers her.

Touch her whole body, with the exception of her breasts and genitals. Avoid these areas. But touching her everywhere else is fine. Again, I want you to touch her as long as is mutually comfortable for both of you.

When you have both touched each other in this way, stop. Go no further. This experience is not to lead to intercourse. You may be thinking, "What? No sex? I thought this was sex therapy!" I urge you to be patient if the process doesn't go as you might have fantasized it.

Many men object to what they call "touchy-feely" experiences of this sort. They say it is just an excuse, used by women who feel uncomfortable, to put off sex. Until the man is willing to look beyond this, and give the exercises a chance, the therapy cannot proceed.

After this experience has been completed once, I ask the couple to do it one more time. Everything should be repeated exactly the same, except that whoever initiated the first experience will be the one to be touched first this time. The one who received first in the initial experience will be the initiator in the second.

The Issues in Step One

Sometimes when a couple return after this exercise, one of them says, "Well, nothing happened. I didn't feel anything." Invariably, we find that the person who says this was expecting some big turn-on or raving sexual experience. That is not the point of this exercise. The only purpose is to provide an opportunity for both participants to experience and become aware of all the more subtle sensations of their sexuality, to become sensual people. This is the quality that is missing in so many long-term sexual relationships. It is all the little sensations that create so much pleasure. When a person becomes so goal-oriented that all he or she thinks about is achieving a big turn on, or having intercourse and subsequent orgasm, that person is going to miss all the little sensations involved. As a result, the degree of sexual pleasure actually enjoyed is greatly reduced.

In this experience, a couple have the opportunity to go back to their adolescence, back to a time when all they could do was to touch or hold hands. Holding hands can be a very erotic experience, if one pays attention to all the little, pleasurable sensations. By giving up the goal of intercourse and orgasm during the touching experience, they are forced to keep their mental focus in the present. They can't go anywhere else, if they stay within the bounds of the therapy. Again, this is similar to adolescent experiences when intercourse was off limits. What many couples discover is that this exercise is extremely sexual, even though intercourse and orgasm are not part of the experience.

Removal of Goals

For the man who is experiencing some type of sexual dysfunction, the removal of the goal of intercourse is a great relief. For example, if he is having problems with erections or premature ejaculation, he will feel relieved that he won't have to perform. His anxiety level will drop dramatically. As a result of his reduction of anxiety, he will be able to relax and to enjoy much more sexual pleasure. Once relaxation occurs, the sexual dysfunction he was experiencing should decrease. Right away, the therapy is structured to break the typical, problematic goal-oriented loop that is associated with most sexual dysfunctions. It is easy to tell someone with sexual dysfunctions to relax and not to worry about the problem, but without a safe structure and strict guidelines to follow, the anxiety will remain.

The outcome of a couple's experience with this exercise tells the therapist as well as the couple a great deal about the degree of intimacy that exists in the relationship. If one or possibly both of the partners have a lot of repressed anger, they will probably report that they didn't feel much when being touched. It is hard to be close to someone you are angry with, even if your anger is repressed or unconscious. Instead of feeling pleasure, they experience being uncomfortable or irritated, because touching makes them aware of their resentments. Since they don't wish to acknowledge the resentments, they repress them and resist the touching experience by numbing their senses.

It becomes obvious to a couple that they are avoiding each other if they somehow are not creating any time to participate in the sex therapy assignments. Usually when this happens, the therapy process changes focus from sex issues to building greater communication and emotional intimacy.

Vulnerability and Control

Another issue this exercise tends to bring to the surface is the ability to be vulnerable in a sexual context. This becomes evident in the reaction of the partner when he or she is on the receiving end of the touch exercise. The person is vulnerable then, because he or she is not in control, except by moving the partner's hand. Otherwise, that partner is in the position of being given a sexual experience without being able to set its tempo, style, or direction. For people who are uncomfortable with being vulnerable in this way, the exercise can be very difficult. They like to be in control of what is occurring in a sexual context. They will have trouble relaxing and keeping themselves from telling their partner how to touch them.

Another indication of difficulty with being vulnerable is that a person responds by being ticklish. Being ticklish to tactile stimulation is a way of guarding yourself from what you perceive as an intrusion. If someone comes up behind you silently and gives you a surprise tickle, you jump and your body tenses. It was a surprise intrusion, and you suddenly felt that you had to guard your body. Ticklishness is a learned response and can be overcome. Often people claim that they are ticklish because they are unusually sensitive; while this may be partly true, the primary cause of ticklishness is fear of vulnerability. It is a symptom rather than a problem in itself.

Beneficial Selfishness

Probably the greatest benefit of this touching exercise is discovering that you can touch your partner for your own pleasure. This idea is very foreign to many people, because it implies selfishness—which has a very negative connotation in our culture. As Dr. Helen Singer Kaplan states in her book, *The New Sex Therapy*, "It is often essential to teach the couple the value of temporary selfishness so that they can lose themselves to the sexual experience." She also says, "To function well sexually, the individual(s) must be able to abandon themselves to the erotic experience."

Being selfish usually implies that you do what you want to, regardless of other people's wishes; this is not what I am recommending when I instruct couples to touch for their own pleasure. I want them to focus on their own pleasure, but not at the expense of their partner's pleasure and sexual experience. This is why the instructions to the receiving partner are to move the hand of the partner if anything is uncomfortable. This is important because it gives the partner who is touching freedom from the worry of pleasing the receiver, and lets the giver have the opportunity to lose him or herself to the sexual experience.

People who have an excessive need to please their partners have difficulty with this exercise, too. To sexually interact for their own pleasure can put them into an emotional bind, allowing them to begin to come to terms with their need to give and to begin accepting pleasure more openly.

Communicating Trust

Another psychological issue that this sexual experience raises is that of trusting that your partner will communicate his/her sexual discomforts. By experiencing the other partner moving your hand to other locations during the sexual exercise, you can learn that your partner can take care of him- or herself. This relieves the anxiety caused by trying to be responsible for your partner's sexual experience.

Through this exercise, the couple build a foundation of trust, allowing both partners to abandon themselves to their own sexual pleasure. This exercise enforces the idea that each partner will take responsibility for his or her own sexuality, freeing both of them to relax and become vulnerable.

Time for Intimacy

Many couples' sexual and/or emotional difficulties stem from the fact that they do not allow time for intimacy. Often the demands of today's lifestyles—two careers, two children, and complex social involvements—don't leave much time even for a couple who aren't experiencing other difficulties. But when problems are present, the couple can be so busy that they don't have much time for each other. They create their busy lifestyle as an unconscious (or in some cases, conscious) attempt to avoid each other, as a coping mechanism. They are trying to maintain a status quo and avoid any intense emotional confrontation. At some level, they may know that they don't have the skills to handle too much intimate contact.

This exercise confronts the problem of time head-on. It forces the couple to look at where they place their time, how they choose to budget it, and where their priorities lie in terms of the importance they place on time alone together. Just creating intimate time together to participate in this exercise may be difficult. They may come back to the next therapy session with all sorts of excuses as to why they couldn't find time to do the home experiences. They may be afraid to do the exercises, but more often I find that they have created routines that simply allow no time for intimacy.

At the point where the couple realize they have literally scheduled sexuality and intimacy out of their lives, they have a choice to either continue in that way or give their sexuality an opportunity to florish. Assuming that they choose the latter, they make a date to spend some intimate time together. Given their lifestyles, they are reminded that this kind of time is not going to appear magically. They have to create it, even if it means sitting down with their calendars and blocking in time for it.

If there are underlying unresolved emotions and issues in their relationship, there may have to be resolved before this exercise is going to be helpful to them.

The Erogenous Body

The last concept that this exercise brings into play is the idea that the whole body is an erogenous zone. By making the breasts and genitals off-limits (usually the main targets of sexual stimulation), they turn their sensual attention to all the other parts of their bodies. They learn that they can derive pleasure from stimulation that doesn't include genital arousal. In this way, they begin to experience the difference between sensual and sexual stimulation.

When a couple's sexuality is goal-oriented, that is, oriented toward orgasm and little if anything in between, this exercise holds quite a few surprises for them. The man may get upset and confused about why his efforts are not leading to intercourse. As often as not, however, after two or three touching experiences, they begin to forget about their sexual goals, focusing instead on the pleasure of the moment, and learning to relax and have fun with sex. Besides learning the pleasure of the moment, they learn new information about their own bodies as well as their partner's. They learn what's pleasurable and what's not. They learn which areas of their bodies are sensitive and which are not.

After completing the first touching exercise, the couple is ready to move on to the next step.

Step Two

In the next step of the therapy, Jane, you are to be the initiator as before, creating a sensual environment. The major difference is that this time when you are touching John's body, you can include his genitals. The idea of touching for your own pleasure still applies. Also, there is still no goal to this experience even though you may be touching his penis. If he gets an erection, fine, but if he doesn't, that is also fine, because that is not the point of the experience. If he ejaculates while you are stimulating him, that is nice for him, but it is not the point of this step in the therapy process.

Another change I would like to make is that when Jane is touching you, John, in addition to moving her hand away from what is not pleasurable, I want you to move her hand in a way that will show her what would be more pleasurable to you. This is a way to show Jane not only what is uncomfortable, but also what gives you the most pleasure. This part of the exercise carries the assumption that Jane finds what you want her to do with her hands pleasurable and comfortable as well. This form of communication and education is essential in learning to be more effective lovers.

When you have touched him for as long as you want, Jane, it is John's turn to touch you, in the same way with all the same instructions in mind. Just because I have said that you can touch her breasts and genitals, John, I don't want you to focus on these areas. Don't forget, the rest of her body has nerve endings too! Again, this exercise is for your own pleasure; you are not trying to achieve any goal or meet any expectation. Just because you can touch Jane's genitals doesn't mean that you should try to give her an orgasm. Touch her genitals because it gives you pleasure. If she happens to have an orgasm, that's nice for her, but that is not the goal. As with the first part of step two, Jane, I want you to move John's hand in a manner that shows what is most pleasurable to you.

This experience is not to include intercourse. This limitation is very important and often you may find it difficult to adhere to, but it is the key to the process. Once John is done touching you, Jane, then the experience is complete. If you both want to talk over what the experience was like for you, that is fine, but only after the actual touching is completed for both of you.

On a separate occasion, John is to be the initiator.

One recommendation I make at this stage of the therapy process is the use of a skin lubricant. I suggest its use only in the genital areas. Given the high concentration of nerve endings there, lubrication will cut down on irritating friction. Skin rubbing on skin in a highly sensitive nerve area is not usually pleasurable. The addition of lubrication will add to the sensuality of the experience. The lubricant I usually recommend goes by the trade name of "Unscented Albolene Liquifying Cleanser." It melts on contact with the skin to the consistency of natural sexual lubricant, but is longer lasting. When making the change from manual stimulation to oral stimulation, Albolene doesn't get in the way because it is completely tasteless. It is intended as a make-up remover and skin moisturizer, so when you go to the drug store to buy some, you won't feel embarrassed because only you know what you are going to be using it for.

The Issues in Step Two

This second step helps the partners provide each other with a map to the territory. By directing their partner as to what gives them pleasure, John and Jane are taking full responsibility for their own sexuality. John is showing Jane how he likes his penis stimulated. The penis is similar to the clitoris, and has various responses to different forms of stimulation. Some areas of the penis are more sensitive than others, and of course this varies from one person to another. Some men like their penis stroked slowly, others fast, or both. Again, it varies from man to man, or even from day to day with the same man. The point of all this is that specific communication is required so that Jane will not be just travelling around aimlessly, lost in sexual territory without a map, an exercise that frustrates both partners.

The communication of specific sexual desires and stimulation is important for both partners, of course. Often it seems the men I see in therapy have very limited knowledge about how to stimu-

218 • *More Than Just Sex*

late their partner's clitoris. Sometimes they aren't even aware of its location.

As with the penis, the clitoris requires different types of stimulation, varying greatly from woman to woman. Some women prefer one side of their clitoris over the other, where others like circling stimulation around the organ. The same woman may want to be stimulated one way in one situation, and another way the next time they make love. So it is important for a woman to communicate to her lover how she wants to be stimulated each time. Just assuming that your partner knows what to do is setting yourself up for frustration.

Ideally, this communication about how she would like to have her genitals stimulated should be given non-verbally, though sometimes a few words may need to be said. Remember, however, that long discourses get in the way of the experience.

The best way for a woman to show a man how she would like her clitoris to be stimulated is for her to place her hand on his and lead him. This is better than telling him verbally, because she is receiving stimulation from him at the same time that she is teaching him. A major issue about sexual responsibility for the man is addressed at this point. This occurs when his partner begins to become more assertive about her specific sexual needs.

Men who are not entirely secure about their sexual confidence and self-esteem may feel threatened and uncomfortable with being instructed by their lover. They may perceive this instruction as a put-down of their sexual ability, and they can become resistant to doing what their partner is asking. Through the therapy process he begins to understand that when his partner gives him information about what pleasures her, it enables him to be a more effective lover. Any man doing this exercise should be reminded before hand that there is no way that he could have known this very specific kind of information without his partner communicating it to him. Regardless of his experience as a lover, only her instructions can tell him what works for her.

Sex Doesn't Equal Intercourse

The next issue that this part of the therapy addresses is being sexual without intercourse. In the first step of the therapy, we are exploring sensuality, or touching for the sake of pleasure. Here we are adding stimulation of the genitals to the sensual experience. For many couples who are experiencing sexual dysfunctions or sexual boredom, this step can be difficult. They are used to feeling that once they become sexually aroused they must immediately commence with intercourse. This step in the therapy blocks that goal-oriented mentality and forces the couple to focus on the pleasure of the moment. It is no accident that many couples compare this experience to make-out sessions they had when they were in high school.

Being able to enjoy sex without having intercourse gives the couple variety and flexibility in their shared sexuality. They can break out of the meat-and-potatoes style of lovemaking. Men who are experiencing problems with premature ejaculation or erection give a sigh of relief when they are told no intercourse. This is especially true for a man who is anxious about controlling his ejaculation. The pressure is lifted from him and he can be sexually involved with his partner—perhaps for the first time. If he does ejaculate before his partner has experienced orgasm, he doesn't have to feel inadequate. He can use other means—his hands or mouth—to stimulate his partner. Added to that, he's almost home in correcting his dysfunction.

For women who are preorgasmic, this stage of the therapy is especially significant. It is critical for her to be able to communicate to her lover the specific forms of sexual stimulation she needs. This stage of the therapy also validates and supports the realization that it is perfectly fine to be orgasmic without intercourse. For women who feel inadequate if they aren't orgasmic while receiving stimulation through intercourse only, this part of the therapy relieves them of some of that anxiety.

Learning to Receive Pleasure

Like the first stage of the process, the second stage puts partners in positions that are emotionally and physically vulnerable. Unlike the first stage, this vulnerability now comes from allowing the partner to touch the most intimate parts of the body. The partner who is being touched is forced to indulge him- or herself in receiving a great deal of intense sexual pleasure. That might sound like heaven to some people, but for others this kind of vulnerability produces more anxiety than pleasure. This is because they have a need to be in control over what is occurring during a sexual experience. This step in the process provides a safe setting for this type of person to better understand his or her fear of losing control. It lets both of them abandon themselves to sexual pleasure.

This is the stage where more traditional counseling techniques may be employed. The roots of a person's fear of sexual vulnerability may need to be examined and understood. Without this insight, their fears are running their lives. Counseling can lead them toward making choices that allow them to both enjoy their sexuality and feel safe, thus surrendering their need for control.

Step Three

After John and Jane have been able to complete and enjoy the first two steps, they are ready to move on to the third.

With this step, Jane, I want you to be the initiator again, except this time both of you are going to touch each other at the same time. It will be the same when John initiates the session.

In this exercise, we reintroduce the intercourse. Jane is to initiate this only when she is ready to have intercourse with John. The recommended position when Jane is ready is with John on his back and Jane on top. During intercourse with Jane, John, should take a passive role. That doesn't mean he should "check out"; rather, relax and enjoy receiving pleasure. In this case, passive simply means not trying to control the experience, unless you (John) are experiencing some discomfort, which you then need to speak up about.

Jane, you should be the one to orchestrate what happens while you and John are having intercourse. You control the rate of first penetration. Once John is inside, just sit there for a moment and let your vagina adjust to John's penis. After this pause, you are free to do whatever is comfortable or pleasurable for you. If you want to move slowly, or if you want to move fast, it is up to you. As was the case with the other steps in the therapy, there is no goal in this step. If orgasms happen for either of you, that is great, but it is not the goal. If one of you doesn't experience an orgasm, there is no failure on anybody's part, as long as you are both feeling pleasure. This experience is to be terminated whenever one of you wants to stop. On another occasion, John, you are to initiate the whole experience, following the same procedure.

The Issues in Step Three

The issues with this step are related to the introduction of intercourse. It is important that Jane initiate intercourse during the pleasuring process, because in most cases the man initiates it, signaled only by his own arousal and his getting an erection. The problem with this is that although he may be ready, his partner may not be. Most men can't recognize when a woman is ready to have intercourse, unless she provides him with very specific signals such as pulling him to her in a way that makes it very clear that this is what she wants. Often the woman consents to intercourse when she isn't ready, just because she feels inadequate at not being as aroused as her partner.

By consenting to intercourse when she is not sufficiently lubricated and aroused, the woman limits the level of sexual pleasure she can experience. It is equivalent to a man trying to have intercourse without an erection—not too much fun! If this pattern of behavior continues on a long-term basis, it may turn her off to intercourse entirely—all without her partner knowing what is happening. As far as he knows, she is enjoying what is occurring and he continues to initiate when ever he is ready. A more experienced man might know better but not unless he had either studied female sexuality or been instructed by a woman. After penetration, it is important for the woman to let her vagina adjust to the penis. The reason for this is that the vagina is relatively closed prior to stimulation. It needs time to relax, expand, and lubricate. Otherwise the woman might experience uncomfortable friction.

Allowing the Woman to Be in Control

With the woman on top in this exercise, and the man relatively passive, the woman has the opportunity to assert herself. With the more common man-on-top position, she is flattened under his weight. He orchestrates the whole experience. He sets the speed and tempo and the depth of penetration. He is in control of the experience because she is not in a position to do much about it.

With the woman on top, she has a chance to express herself. She can do whatever is pleasurable for her. Alexandra Penny states in her book *How to Make Love to a Man*, "Some women say that they are reluctant to suggest this position because they feel they might appear overly aggressive. On the contrary, for many men this is the most erotic way to make love." In this position she is able to give herself or her partner additional manual stimulation, or her partner can give either or both of them stimulation from below. This could definitely increase pleasure over intercourse by itself, something that can be especially important for a woman who doesn't experience orgasms through intercourse alone, and would like to experience orgasm while having intercourse with her partner.

By remaining passive, the man learns to relinquish control and allow himself to be vulnerable. For some men, this is no problem; but for others, losing control can be threatening. In the latter case, the man can learn to lay back and receive the pleasure he is experiencing during this step in the therapy process. If he has trouble participating at this point, then the therapist can help him explore the fears he may be experiencing. This therapy might include traditional insight therapy with a behavioral process of confrontation, taking what is learned from the verbal part of the therapy and applying it to actual behavior.

As an aside, the female-astride position is also very useful when the man is working on his ejaculation control. It allows him to control the level of stimulation because he can signal to his partner to pull off when he is coming close to ejaculating. Also, he has gravity on his side. When he is on top, he has to tighten up to support his body. In the female-astride position, this is not the case. His entire body can be at rest except for his erect penis. This ability to physically relax is an essential component in controlling the timing of his ejaculation.

Step Four

By this point in the therapeutic process, John and Jane have integrated some of the major concepts of this book. They have broken and changed whatever sexual patterns that may have trapped them.

The last step for John and Jane is to do whatever you are comfortable with doing, in whatever order or sequence you choose, and for however long. The purpose of the therapy is not to set up another rigid pattern. The idea is to be creative and free, to mix all the steps you have learned— for example, a little general body touching, some missionary-style intercourse, a little genital touching, and then back to intercourse using a different position.

Now that the level of pleasure has been increased, I might suggest that the partners talk to one another a little more during sexual experience. For some, this can be just as exciting as touch.

The point is never to follow the same pattern twice. Instead of playing the same five notes over and over in the same order, you now have a full range of notes, and the combinations are endless.

224 • *More Than Just Sex*

Instead of playing a half-hearted duet, you're now able to enjoy a full orchestra!

This might sound somewhat corny, but I think I have figured out where the metaphor of fireworks comes from, as applied to sex. A good fireworks show is just one beautiful explosion after another. When they have no rigid pattern, the couple have the freedom to be inventive and spontaneous. Their sexual experience becomes one fantastic pleasuring activity after another. The trick is to make it last. Like rich food, you can only have so much of it, but your mind still wants more. This is the way I hope you view your own sexual relationship.

Conclusion

Once the couple have mastered the mechanics of sex, the technology, the next order of business is to come back to the fundamental question of feelings. How do you feel about your partner? How do you feel about yourself? Do you like what you are doing? These are much tougher questions than questions of technique, because they are about how we experience life, not just how we do sexual things.

"Ours is a culture that makes figuring out how to be physically sexual so complicated that many people never get to the question of how they feel about it," says John Gagnon in his book *Human Sexuality.* The key to long-term sexual fulfillment in a relationship is not usually what physical position a couple uses, or what sexual technique they employ, but what their feelings or emotions are toward each other. The way a couple interact physically is important but it plays a secondary role to their emotional interactions. Every therapist has known at least one divorcing couple who said, "Oh, the sex was fine, but that's all we had between us. It wasn't enough."

When they are talking about their sex lives, most couples use the word "love" to describe how they feel. However, being emotionally involved or "in love" with a long-term partner doesn't mean that you are only going to experience warm, affectionate feelings. A committed relationship involves all the emotions of the human experience. Anger and related emotions are very important to the quality and intensity of a couple's sexual experience.

The repression, denial, or avoidance of anger is a sure ticket to the sexual doldrums. With so many couples the primary reason they have turned from lovers into roommates is that they have repressed resentments and hurts in their relationship. When this happens, it takes a lot more than changing rooms to go from being roommates back to being lovers.

The key for any couple that want to have more than just sex in their life is to find constructive ways to communicate—both the easy and the difficult emotions. Open communication may not be the only component in a good sex life, but it's way ahead of whatever is in second place.

Sexual Perception Inventory

This questionnaire is a handy tool for a couple to use in helping them get a picture of how both of them view their sexual relationship. Their individual perceptions may be similar, or very different, but they are both right.

This questionnaire is not a test to be scored or judged. It is just a way to help a couple verbally communicate about a subject that tends to be very difficult. It also helps them discover any false assumptions that they may have.

Instructions

The questionnaire is to be answered by each individual partner separately. No comparing answers until both have finished completely. Then the couple can compare their answers and discuss their reactions. When the questions require a "time" answer, just give your approximate estimation, please, no clock watching or stopwatches.

1. How frequently do you and your partner have sexual intercourse?
    - ☐ more than once a day
    - ☐ once a day
    - ☐ 3 or 4 times a week
    - ☐ twice a week
    - ☐ once a week
    - ☐ once every two weeks
    - ☐ once a month
    - ☐ less than once a month
    - ☐ not at all

2. How frequently would you like to have sexual intercourse?
    - ☐ more than once a day
    - ☐ once a day
    - ☐ 3 or 4 times a week
    - ☐ twice a week

    ☐ once a week
    ☐ once every two weeks
    ☐ once a month
    ☐ less than once a month

3. How frequently do you think your partner would like to have sexual intercourse?
    ☐ more than once a day
    ☐ once a day
    ☐ 3 or 4 times a week
    ☐ twice a week
    ☐ once a week
    ☐ once every two weeks
    ☐ once a month
    ☐ less than once a month

4. Who usually initiates having sexual intercourse?
    ☐ I always do
    ☐ I usually do
    ☐ my partner and I each initiate about equally often
    ☐ my partner usually does
    ☐ my partner always does

5. Who would you like to have initiate sexual intercourse?
    ☐ myself, always
    ☐ myself, usually
    ☐ my partner and I equally often
    ☐ my partner usually
    ☐ my partner always

6. When your partner makes sexual advances, how do you usually respond?
    ☐ usually with pleasure
    ☐ sometimes accept with pleasure
    ☐ sometimes accept reluctantly
    ☐ usually accept reluctantly
    ☐ often refuse
    ☐ usually refuse

7. When you make sexual advances, how does your partner respond?
    - ☐ usually accepts with pleasure
    - ☐ sometimes accepts with pleasure
    - ☐ sometimes accepts reluctantly
    - ☐ usually accepts reluctantly
    - ☐ often refuses
    - ☐ usually refuses

8. Are you able to ask your partner to give you sexual pleasure in specific ways?
    - ☐ nearly always, over 90% of the time
    - ☐ usually, about 75% of the time
    - ☐ sometimes, about 50% of the time
    - ☐ seldom, about 25% of the of the time
    - ☐ rarely, less than 10% of the time
    - ☐ never
    - ☐ have never tried to

9. Is your partner able to ask you for sexual pleasure in specific ways?
    - ☐ nearly always, over 90% of the time
    - ☐ usually, about 75% of the time
    - ☐ sometimes, about 50% of the time
    - ☐ seldom, about 25% of the of the time
    - ☐ rarely, less than 10% of the time
    - ☐ never

10. How comfortable are you in asking your partner to give you sexual pleasure in specific ways during lovemaking?
    - ☐ very comfortable
    - ☐ moderately comfortable
    - ☐ slightly comfortable
    - ☐ slightly uncomfortable
    - ☐ moderately uncomfortable
    - ☐ very uncomfortable
    - ☐ not sure; I haven't tried

230 • *More Than Just Sex*

11. How comfortable do you think your partner is about asking you for sexual pleasure in specific ways during lovemaking?
    - ☐ very comfortable
    - ☐ moderately comfortable
    - ☐ slightly comfortable
    - ☐ slightly uncomfortable
    - ☐ moderately uncomfortable
    - ☐ very uncomfortable
    - ☐ not sure; partner hasn't tried

12. How does your partner respond to such specific requests during lovemaking?
    - ☐ very positively
    - ☐ somewhat positively
    - ☐ neutrally, but goes along with my requests
    - ☐ somewhat negatively, but usually goes along with my request
    - ☐ somewhat negatively, usually ignores requests
    - ☐ very negatively

13. How do you respond when your partner makes specific requests during lovemaking?
    - ☐ very positively
    - ☐ somewhat negatively, but usually go along with such requests somewhat positively
    - ☐ somewhat negatively; I usually ignore such requests
    - ☐ neutrally but I usually go along with such requests
    - ☐ very negatively

14. How long do you and your partner usually engage in sexual foreplay (kissing, petting, etc.) before having intercourse?
    - ☐ less than one minute
    - ☐ 1 to 3 minutes
    - ☐ 4 to 6 minutes
    - ☐ 7 to 10 minutes
    - ☐ 11 to 15 minutes
    - ☐ 16 to 30 minutes
    - ☐ 30 minutes to an hour
    - ☐ more than an hour

15. How long would you like to engage in sexual foreplay before having intercourse?
    - ☐ less than one minute
    - ☐ 1 to 3 minutes
    - ☐ 4 to 6 minutes
    - ☐ 7 to 10 minutes
    - ☐ 11 to 15 minutes
    - ☐ 16 to 30 minutes
    - ☐ 30 minutes to an hour
    - ☐ more than an hour

16. How long do you think that your partner would like to engage in sexual foreplay before having intercourse?
    - ☐ less than one minute
    - ☐ 1 to 3 minutes
    - ☐ 4 to 6 minutes
    - ☐ 7 to 10 minutes
    - ☐ 11 to 15 minutes
    - ☐ 16 to 30 minutes
    - ☐ 30 minutes to an hour
    - ☐ more than an hour

17. How long does intercourse usually last from entry of the penis until the male reaches orgasm (climax)?
    - ☐ ejaculation occurs before entry
    - ☐ ejaculation occurs during entry
    - ☐ less than 10 seconds
    - ☐ 10 seconds to 1 minute
    - ☐ 1 to 3 minutes
    - ☐ 3 to 5 minutes
    - ☐ 5 to 10 minutes
    - ☐ 10 to 20 minutes
    - ☐ more than 20 minutes

18. How long would you like intercourse to last?
    - ☐ ejaculation occurs before entry
    - ☐ ejaculation occurs during entry
    - ☐ less than 10 seconds

☐ 10 seconds to 1 minute
☐ 1 to 3 minutes
☐ 3 to 5 minutes
☐ 5 to 10 minutes
☐ 10 to 20 minutes
☐ more than 20 minutes

19. How long do you think your partner would like intercourse to last?
☐ ejaculation occurs before entry
☐ ejaculation occurs during entry
☐ less than 10 seconds
☐ 10 seconds to 1 minute
☐ 1 to 3 minutes
☐ 3 to 5 minutes
☐ 5 to 10 minutes
☐ 10 to 20 minutes
☐ more than 20 minutes

20. If you try, is it possible for you to reach orgasm through having your genitals caressed by your partner?
☐ nearly always, over 90% of the time
☐ usually, about 75% of the time
☐ sometimes, about 50% of the time
☐ seldom, about 25% of the time
☐ rarely, less than 10% of the time
☐ never

21. MEN: If you try, is it possible for you to reach orgasm through sexual intercourse?
☐ nearly always, over 90% of the time
☐ usually, about 75% of the time
☐ sometimes, about 50% of the time
☐ seldom, about 25% of the time
☐ rarely, less than 10% of the time
☐ never

22. WOMEN: If you try, is it possible for you to reach orgasm through sexual intercourse with simultaneous clitoral stimulation?

☐ nearly always, over 90% of the time
☐ usually, about 75% of the time
☐ sometimes, about 50% of the time
☐ seldom, about 25% of the time
☐ rarely, less than 10% of the time
☐ never

23. WOMEN: Is it possible for you to reach orgasm through sexual intercourse alone without additional stimulation?
☐ nearly always, over 90% of the time
☐ usually, about 75% of the time
☐ sometimes, about 50% of the time
☐ seldom, about 25% of the time
☐ rarely, less than 10% of the time
☐ never

24. Does the man have any trouble in getting an erection before intercourse begins?
☐ never
☐ rarely, less than 10% of the time
☐ seldom, about 25% of the time
☐ sometimes, about 50% of the time
☐ usually, about 75% of the time
☐ nearly always, over 90% of the time

25. Does the man have any trouble keeping an erection, once intercourse has begun?
☐ never
☐ rarely, less than 10% of the time
☐ seldom, about 25% of the time
☐ sometimes, about 50% of the time
☐ usually, about 75% of the time
☐ nearly always, over 90% of the time

26. How often do you masturbate?
☐ more than once a day
☐ once a day
☐ 3 or 4 times a week
☐ twice a week
☐ once a week

☐ once every two weeks
☐ once a month
☐ less than once a month
☐ not at all

27. If you try, is it possible for you to reach orgasm through masturbation?
☐ nearly always, over 90% of the time
☐ usually, about 75% of the time
☐ sometimes, about 50% of the time
☐ seldom, about 25% of the time
☐ rarely, less than 10% of the time
☐ never

28. How long does it take before you reach orgasm through masturbation?
☐ less than one minute
☐ 2 to 5 minutes
☐ 5 to 10 minutes
☐ 10 to 20 minutes
☐ 20 to 30 minutes
☐ more than 30 minutes
☐ stop without reaching orgasm

29. How frequently do you have erotic fantasies during masturbation?
☐ nearly always, over 90% of the time
☐ usually, about 75% of the time
☐ sometimes, about 50% of the time
☐ seldom, about 25% of the time
☐ rarely, less than 10% of the time
☐ never

30. How frequently do you have erotic fantasies during lovemaking with your partner?
☐ nearly always, over 90% of the time
☐ usually, about 75% of the time
☐ sometimes, about 50% of the time
☐ seldom, about 25% of the time

☐ rarely, less than 10% of the time
☐ never

31. Estimate the percentage of times you use the following techniques in masturbation. Underline your preferred method(s).
WOMEN:
☐ manual clitoral stimulation
☐ vibrator
☐ running water
☐ pressure; squeezing legs together
☐ rubbing or moving against something
☐ inserting fingers or object into vagina
☐ stimulating parts of the body other than the genital area
☐ using pornographic or erotic material
☐ other (specify)
MEN:
☐ manual stimulation without lubrication
☐ manual stimulation with lubrication
☐ stimulating part of the body other than the penis
☐ rubbing the penis against something—e.g., sheet or pillow
☐ inserting the penis into something (specify)
☐ using pornographic or erotic material
☐ other (specify)

32. What is your usual reaction to erotic or pornographic materials (pictures, movies, books)?
☐ greatly aroused
☐ somewhat aroused
☐ not aroused
☐ negative, embarrassed, repulsed, etc.

33. Overall, how satisfactory to you is your sexual relationship with your partner?
☐ extremely unsatisfactory
☐ moderately unsatisfactory
☐ slightly unsatisfactory
☐ slightly satisfactory

☐ moderately satisfactory
☐ extremely satisfactory
☐ other (specify)

34. Overall, how satisfactory do you think your sexual relationship is to your partner?
☐ extremely unsatisfactory
☐ moderately unsatisfactory
☐ slightly unsatisfactory
☐ slightly satisfactory
☐ moderately satisfactory
☐ extremely satisfactory
☐ other (specify)

35. List three things about your own sexual behavior that you would most like to change:
1.
2.
3.

36. List three things about your partner's sexual behavior that you would most like to see changed:
1.
2.
3.

37. Using the following scale
1. extremely pleasurable
2. moderately pleasurable
3. mildly pleasurable
4. neutral or indifferent
5. mildly unpleasant
6. moderately unpleasant
7. extremely unpleasant

rate the following activities for yourself. Then rate how you think your partner would rate them.
1. seeing yourself nude   Self____ Partner____
2. seeing your partner nude   Self____ Partner____

3. being seen nude by your partner Self____ Partner____
4. affectionate cuddling Self____ Partner____
5. kissing Self____ Partner____
6. giving a body massage, not including breasts or genitals
   Self____ Partner____
7. getting a body massage, not including breasts or genitals
   Self____ Partner____
8. the man pleasuring the woman's breasts with his hands
   Self____ Partner____
9. the man pleasuring the woman's genitals with his hands
   Self____ Partner____
10. the man pleasuring the woman's genitals to orgasm
    with his hands Self____ Partner____
11. the woman pleasuring the man's breasts with her hands
    Self____ Partner____
12. the woman pleasuring the man's genitals with her
    hands Self____ Partner____
13. the woman pleasuring the mans genitals to orgasm
    with her hands Self____ Partner____
14. the man orally pleasuring the woman's genitals
    Self____ Partner____
15. the man orally pleasuring the woman's genitals to
    orgasm Self____ Partner____
16. the woman orally pleasuring the man's genitals
    Self____ Partner____
17. the woman orally pleasuring the man's genitals to
    orgasm Self____ Partner____
18. intercourse—penetration and slow movement
    Self____ Partner____
19. intercourse—penetration and rapid thrusting
    Self____ Partner____
20. pleasuring of the woman's breasts during intercourse
    Self____ Partner____
21. pleasuring of the woman's clitoris during intercourse
    Self____ Partner____
22. pleasuring of the man's breasts during intercourse
    Self____ Partner____

23. orgasm during intercourse for the woman

Self____ Partner____

24. orgasm during intercourse for the man

Self____ Partner____

25. lovemaking in which both partners are aroused and the woman does not have orgasm   Self____ Partner____

26. lovemaking in which both partners are aroused and the man does not have orgasm   Self____ Partner____

27. lovemaking in which the woman is relaxed and inactive   Self____ Partner____

28. lovemaking in which the man is relaxed and inactive

Self____ Partner____

29. affectionate physical contact with a member of the same sex   Self____ Partner____

30. sexual contact with a member of the same sex

Self____ Partner____

31. masturbation   Self____ Partner____

32. erotic fantasy   Self____ Partner____

Bibliography

Barbach, Lonnie, Ph.D. *For Each Other: Sharing Sexual Intimacy.* Garden City, New York: Doubleday, 1988.

Barbach, Lonnie. *For Yourself: The Fulfillment of Female Sexuality.* Garden City, New York: Doubleday, 1976.

Botwin, Carol. *Is There Sex After Marriage?* Boston: Little Brown, 1985.

Brauer, Alan, M.D., and Brauer, Donna. *ESO.* New York: Warner Books, 1989.

Castleman, Michael. *Sexual Solutions: An Information Guide.* New York: Simon & Schuster, 1980.

Comfort, Alex. *More Joy.* New York: Crown Publishers, 1973.

Gagnon, John. *Human Sexualities.* New York: Scott Foresman, 1977.

Greene, Gael. *Delicious Sex.* New York: Bantam Books, 1988.

Kaplan, Helen Singer. *Disorders of Sexual Desire.* New York: Brunner-Mazel, 1979.

Kaplan, Helen Singer. *The New Sex Therapy.* New York: Brunner-Mazel, 1974.

Kassorla, Irene. *Nice Girls Do.* New York: Berkley, 1984.

Masters, William H., and Johnson, Virginia E. *Human Sexual Response.* Boston: Little Brown, 1966.

Montague, Ashley. *Touching: The Human Significance of the Skin,* 2nd ed. New York: Harper & Row, 1978.

Penney, Alexandra. *How to Make Love to a Man.* New York: Dell, 1982.

Phillips, Debora. *Sexual Confidence: Discovering the Joys of Intimacy.* Boston: Houghton Mifflin, 1985.

Satir, Virginia. *Peoplemaking.* New York: Science and Behavior, 1972.

Zilbergeld, Bernie, Ph.D. *Male Sexuality.* Boston: Little Brown, 1978.

Living at the Heart of Creation
by Michael Exeter

Living at the Heart of Creation is not a self-help manual or a "fix-it" book of superficial answers. It is, rather, an intelligent yet simple offering of insight into such challenging areas as the environmental crises, overpopulation, business relationships, and personal well-being. Michael Exeter shows exactly what it means to live at the heart of creation—to live at the place T. S. Eliot called "the still point of the turning world."

This book will be a friend and companion to anyone with the desire to explore what it means to be vibrant and wise in these extraordinary times.

$9.95

Gentle Roads to Survival
by Andre Auw, Ph.D.

Psychologist Andre Auw, a close associate of great 20th-century psychologists Carl Rogers and Virginia Satir, characterizes people who learn to prevail over life's challenges as survivors. While some are born survivors, for most of us, survival is a skill that must be learned. Using dozens of case histories, poems, and allegories, Auw identifies the lessons all survivors know: characteristics that distinguish people who give up hope from those who find the inspiration and encouragement to carry on.

"I loved your ideas. They contain a great deal of wisdom, wisdom gained from experience."   *—Carl Rogers*

$9.95

Your Body Believes Every Word You Say
by Barbara Levine

This is the first book to describe the language of the link between the mind and body. Barbara Levine's fifteen-year battle with a huge brain tumor led her to trace common phrases like "that breaks my heart" and "it's a pain in the butt" back to the underlying beliefs on which they were based and the symptoms they cause. She lists hundreds of common examples of words we use unconsciously every day, and shows how these "seedthoughts" can set us up for illness.

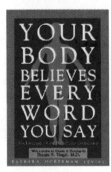

$11.95

Personal Power Cards
by Barbara Gress

A simple, easy to use set of flash cards for emotional wellness. Includes 55 cards, a carrying pouch, and an 80 page booklet. The Cards help retrain your feelings to be positive and healthy. Their combination of colors, shapes, and words allow positive thoughts to penetrate deep into your subconscious, "programming" your emotions for health.

"In the twenty years I have been using color and mind imagery with patients, I have never seen any approach have such a great benefit on self-discipline and self-esteem."
—Richard Shames, M.D.
Family Practitioner and author of Healing with Mind Power

$18.95

Voices From the Womb

by Michael Gabriel with Marie Gabriel

This is the first book to use extensive hypnotic regression to reveal the actual experiences of infants while in the womb. It shows that unborn infants are far more conscious and aware than has previously been recognized.

Michael Gabriel's exciting, unprecedented work traces the experiences of infants from the moment of conception through birth. It shows how deeply affected they are by their parents and the emotional harmony or confusion of adults.

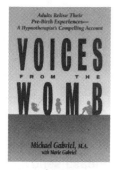

$9.95

Magnificent Addiction

by Philip R. Kavanaugh, M.D.

This book will decisively change the way you see addictions—forever. From the unique vantage point of a physician who has treated thousands of patients with emotional disorders, yet has undergone a major life-breakdown and healing himself, this revolutionary book takes all the assumptions that our society has about diagnosis and treatment and turns them upside down.

Speaking not as a detached clinical observer but as one who has gone through the painful and difficult experiences that life can bring, Dr. Kavanaugh forcefully argues for passionate addiction to life itself. The pages of this book sing with the power and purpose of a new and exciting message: that our most severe emotional crises are the very agents that stimulate us to reach for our highest good.

$12.95

Winds Across the Sky

by Chris Foster

Every so often a novel comes along that is simple, magical, utterly unique and compelling. *Winds Across the Sky* is that kind of rare, exceptional work. Woven around the themes of ecology, recovery, male-female relationships, and other great issues of the day, Chris Foster's lean prose and poetic style make this a book that pierces the heart of the reader.

This book portrays the fundamental unity of all creation in a new way and across a broader spectrum. It portrays loving communication as it occurs easily between different species and between humans and the natural world. Through tragedy and defeat, it potently affirms life's goodness and the inherent oneness of all creation.

$12.95 Hardback

Magic at our Hand

by Nancy Rose Exeter

Nancy Exeter, in a book which is as much a work of art as a work of prose, here expertly touches the essence of the universal feminine. With a gentle, clear voice, she calls every person to an awareness of the exquisite beauty to be found in every moment if we can only be aware. This book will inspire you, and prompt you to look on the world around you with the eyes of a child.

$11.95

Order Form

(Please print legibly)   Date _____

Name _____

Address _____

City _____ State _____ Zip _____

Phone _____

Please send a catalog to my friend:

Name _____

Address _____

City _____ State _____ Zip _____

Quantity Discounts!

$2 off if you order 2 items
$3 off if you order 3 items
$4 off if you order 4 items, etc...

Item	Qty.	Price	Amount
More Than Just Sex		$12.95	
Living at the Heart of Creation		$9.95	
Gentle Roads to Survival		$9.95	
Your Body Believes Every Word You Say		$11.95	
Personal Power Cards		$18.95	
Voices From the Womb		$9.95	
Magnificent Addiction		$12.95	
Winds Across the Sky		$12.95	
Magic at Our Hand		$11.95	

Add for shipping:

Book Rate: $2.50 for first item, $1.00 for ea. add. item.
First Class/UPS: $4.00 for first item, $1.50 ea. add. item.
Canada/Mexico: One-and-a-half times shipping rates.
Overseas: Double shipping rates.

Subtotal	
Quantity Discount	
Calif. res. add 7.25% sales tax	
Shipping	
Grand Total	

Check type of payment:

☐ Check or money order enclosed

☐ Visa ☐ MasterCard

Acct. # _____

Exp. Date _____

Signature _____

Send order to:
Aslan Publishing
PO Box 108
Lower Lake, CA 95457
or call to order:
(800) 275-2606

MJS

Order Form

(Please print legibly)   Date _____

Name _____

Address _____

City _____ State _____ Zip _____

Phone _____

Please send a catalog to my friend:

Name _____

Address _____

City _____ State _____ Zip _____

Quantity Discounts!

$2 off if you order 2 items
$3 off if you order 3 items
$4 off if you order 4 items, etc...

Item	Qty.	Price	Amount
More Than Just Sex		$12.95	
Living at the Heart of Creation		$9.95	
Gentle Roads to Survival		$9.95	
Your Body Believes Every Word You Say		$11.95	
Personal Power Cards		$18.95	
Voices From the Womb		$9.95	
Magnificent Addiction		$12.95	
Winds Across the Sky		$12.95	
Magic at Our Hand		$11.95	

Add for shipping:
Book Rate: $2.50 for first item, $1.00 for ea. add. item.
First Class/UPS: $4.00 for first item, $1.50 ea. add. item.
Canada/Mexico: One-and-a-half times shipping rates.
Overseas: Double shipping rates.

Subtotal	
Quantity Discount	
Calif. res. add 7.25% sales tax	
Shipping	
Grand Total	

Check type of payment:

☐ Check or money order enclosed

☐ Visa ☐ MasterCard

Acct. # _____

Exp. Date _____

Signature _____

Send order to:
Aslan Publishing
PO Box 108
Lower Lake, CA 95457
or call to order:
(800) 275-2606

MJS